THE STRANGER ON THE THRESHOLD

ESSAYS AND STORIES ON LOVE AND COMPASSION

Including: THE OAK ON THE PLAIN
AND
THE ALLOTMENT

BY PAUL BURA

paul@paulbura.co.uk
paulbura@supanet.com

Published by
THE BOSGO PRESS

First published 2003
Copyright © Paul Bura 2003
Editing and layout by Sidney Smiles
Photograph by Frank Youngs
Cover illustration by Hanne Jahr
This book cannot be reproduced in any form, either in part or total without express permission from the author.
ISBN 0 906786 28 2
Previous books by Paul Bura:
Just Another Poet
Mustn't Dent The Memory
Behind The Joker
From Under The Stairs
The Coming Of The Giants
The Space Between The Syllables
In The End Love Is All There Is
The Oak On The Plain
Joeb – Servant of Gaia
Quest For Contact
The Drunk On The Train
Brand New
Stepping To The Drummer
And Love Said: The Oracle

Other books by Paul Bura please email:
paulbura@supanet.com
or write to the
address below C/O Paul Bura

Published by
THE BOSGO PRESS
12, Gongl Rhedyn,
Cemaes Bay, Anglesey LL67 OHY. UK

<u>DEDICATION</u>
AND LOVE SAID:
I will pursue you till
The end of time and
Beyond. You will
Never shake me off.
I will be the shadow at
High Noon that you
Never see,
The witness of all that
You say and do.
Until one day you embrace me as your equal.

AND COMPASSION SAID:
I am the companion of love,
The manifestation and the doer;
The forgiver and the healer;
Those of you who choose
To walk the path of compassion
Must first accomplish <u>love</u>
And recognition of the Infinite.
(Anon)

CONTENTS...
PREFACE by Jan and Mike Pendragon.

1. The Healer on the Bridge.
8. The Bosham Stone.
13. Playing Dumb.
18. The Allotment.
33. The Seeds.
40. The Stooping Goddess.
46. The Oak on the Plain.
71. Pushing Time.
75. Stone Circles in Sudbury.
89. The Stranger on the Threshold.
93. Love Is All There Is.
96. Karma.
99. Journey from Alpha to Omega and... back.
103. Infinite Humour.
109. Idle Hands.
113. Freedom.
117. Forgiveness.
121. Epilepsy.
130. The Blue Pond.
140. Finding the Balance.
142. Do Not Follow Where the Path May Lead.
145. Don't Trust Me I'm a Psychic.
152. Circles of Change.

PREFACE

A few years ago, whilst living in Manchester, we came across an article in a magazine, which moved us so deeply, that we knew we just had to make contact with the author. Through his words, this writer reached out and touched not only our minds, but our hearts and souls as well. However, all our enquiries led to a dead end, and we couldn't track him down anywhere.

A few months went by, and we spent a holiday on Anglesey, staying with a couple who just happened to mention that their friend's brother was an amazing person – a writer with the most wonderful voice, who lived just a few miles away. Of course, you've guessed it – it turned out to be the writer we were so eager to make contact with!

*The writer in question was Paul Bura, and since then, we have read all his books, and have had the privilege of publishing some of his articles and poems in our magazine **"One Vision"**. We have also become very good friends, and he has graced us with his presence at some of our weekend seminars, as a guest poet, and always receiving a tremendous reception.*

*What can we say about Paul Bura? He writes from his soul, from the very depths of his being, and if ever a man was gifted, he is. With his words he can transport us from laughter to tears in a matter of moments, for he has the wonderful ability to allow us to see, and also feel, the world through his eyes. Paul understands so well our vulnerabilities as well as our strengths, our human-ness, as well as our divinity. He tells our stories **for** us, verbalising the feelings that we sometimes just can't adequately express in words ourselves.*

This latest book is a collection of essays, articles and stories, that will make you laugh, cry, and experience every other emotion in between. It will inspire, encourage, and uplift you, and leave you feeling that the world truly is a better place, for Paul Bura being in it.

*We thank him for sharing his gift with the world, and for the love, light and laughter that he radiates out to others, which is the very essence of **who we really are**. And thank him too, for showing us the real meaning of 'courage', for he has displayed tremendous courage throughout his life, in the face of adversity. He truly is a giant amongst men.*

Jan and Mike Pendragon: "ONE VISION"

THE HEALER ON THE BRIDGE

I moved to Anglesey from Sussex to be near my family. My sister Josie had moved there (from Sussex) about a year before. My younger sister Melly and her husband Frank and two boys, had bought a large, rambling house called *The Firs* (see Ordnance Survey Map of Anglesey, extreme North) on Anglesey about a year before and were in the process of 'doing it up' and opening up the house (and considerable grounds) for *bed n' breakfast*. Josie was invited to stay with them in her own small 'upstairs' apartment, and was soon joined by my nephew Quenton, Josie's son. My brother Kevin and his wife Maureen also lived in West Wales.

You can see that, all in all, my mother and I were obligated to do the same. Incidentally, my mother *hates* it here because it's so remote and far from the madding crowd. She's a shopping kind of person and takes great pleasure in 'window shopping', her cheeks bulging with sweets or toffees, an idiosyncratic habit of hers that has been with her since her youth, and anyway (she says) the 'hills get under her feet'.

Well, that kind of sets the scene for what was to follow.

Before I left Sussex I was a sort of *'trainer or coach'* in the psychic arts: teaching folk about the art of 'seeing' and 'communication'. Toward the end of my time in Sussex I too was having trouble communicating with my *own* speech, my *physical* speech.

To cut a very long story to ribbons: when I arrived in Wales it was only a month or so before I had my first 'fit', then another. I was diagnosed with a meningioma (a tumour on the brain about the size of an orange. They did not specify what size of orange: a Jaffa or the smaller Spanish variety!). They removed it at the *Walton Hospital for Neurology* in Liverpool. After a few complications they sent me home to recuperate. It was then that I first met him: *The Healer on the Bridge!*

I always make a habit of greeting the Guardian of a place, whether it is a sacred area of power, a wood, field, or an ancient church. They *always* have their Guardians, without exception. A place will always fall into the embrace of *some* Guardian or other (the area is normally *triangular* in shape, well in my own experience it is). The ancient *Hill Fort* of *Cissbury* in Sussex has *three* Guardians, Emun, Rachael and Tryst, this being an exception to the rule (so far). *Wolstonbury Hill* has one Guardian, Damus, a Druid. Or 'Drood', as Damus told me, relating to the collective, as there were many types and many tribes.

Guardians work closely with the *devic forces* but in no way 'control' them. The devas' work *with* them and not *for* them. On the whole the devic forces (elementals) do not trust human beings, and who can blame them? Most human beings spread poison on the land in their ignorance: 'Oh nature can cope, nature can adapt'. Human beings are brought up 'blind' to what is around them. They are taught from infancy to be blind. Devas work with the Guardians because they *choose* to do so, knowing that in them they have an ally, someone they can trust. A Guardian's work is primarily to do with *earth maintenance,* keeping the energy lines clear. Though their job is becoming harder as human beings continue to deny them, to deny that they even exist! Mind you, I cannot imagine teaching a class of kids about Guardians: "Right children, today we are going to talk about Guardians. Of course you cannot actually *see* them, but they are there, none-the-less..." Oh I don't know though. Perhaps it *would* work? Angelic beings are taught in schools where religious instruction is given, and you can't *see* them! Well, only the privileged few.

As I have previously stated, I always make a habit of greeting the Guardian of a place. In *Cemaes Bay,* Anglesey, where I live, there runs through the village a little river called the *Wygyr* (pronounced 'Wigear'). It runs lazily through a little wooded area where once ran a small steam tram. Remains of the 'track' can still be seen. I can never quite understand why folk don't take more advantage of this little piece of tranquillity. Apart from the odd walker it remains, on the whole, deserted.

As I made my way down the steep pathway that leads from the main A5025 road, I directed my thought in a greeting. Instantly there came back a reply! "Greetings to you too, my friend. It's been a long time since anyone has spoken to me. In your terms maybe two or three hundred years." Now I'd had considerable experience with Guardians but never such a quick response as this! I asked him about his work here and he directed me to an area where an energy line (*Courier Line: Giver and Receiver of information*) ran through a section of river, the water tumbling and swirling into a pool before making its ultimate journey to the sea. "There is an energy spiral here!" He pointed. "I can *feel* it!" I replied. I understood from him that he keeps the energy lines clear in Cemaes, or tries to.

The Guardians name is *Cydwr*, a Druid (no surprise there!). He stands no more than 5 foot 6 inches. He wears a robe of rough cloth that has a headpiece that comes down to his shoulders, tied around the forehead. He is rotund, cutting a Friar

Tuck figure. In his right hand he holds a staff made of plain wood, not carved in any way. "Do you require healing?" "Why yes, " I replied, "are you a healer too?" "Some say," he said, "but I require that you stand on the bridge. I work better over flowing water, the energy generated from flowing water over rocks is all-important." (Later on I learned that the negative dross from whoever is undergoing the healing, is carried away and out to sea, where it is purified once again.) I made my way to one of the little bridges that span the river, the one nearest the High Street in Cemaes, the one where the mouth of the river gently bites the sea. I stopped midway and closed my eyes. At this stage it must be pointed out that I never respond to healers in the usual way, whoever they happen to be. I don't feel heat. I don't feel a tingling sensation. None of that. But I *do* feel relaxed. It was the same with Cydwr (pronounced Cuddoor with a slight roll of the tongue). But I *do* feel *very* relaxed.

Through the months that followed I was receiving healing every time that I went down to this little piece of paradise. Almost ever day, in fact! I was also receiving healing from a local healer (Margaret) who came once a week to my home. I needed all the help I could get.

But was it Cydwr or the local healer, or a combination of the two? I came to the conclusion that it was the latter. Cydwr worked more on my mental, rather than my physical, self.

I had visitors, a couple from the South of England, a couple of my old students. I took them down to meet Cydwr. They at once felt his presence, his warmth of welcome. I said to Jim, who was having trouble with his lower back, to stand on the bridge and let Cydwr do his stuff. After a couple of minutes he felt a warmth in his back: "Something's happening," he said, "the pain is subsiding. He came away feeling considerably better. The pain had vanished!

Another of my ex-students, a student with the gift of *seeing*, described him in every detail, without any prompting from me, exactly as I had seen him. She even found the *spiral of energy* cascading out from the cluster of rocks that connected to the Courier Line, again, without any prompting from me.

The Healer of the Bridge is a reality. Go to him with your aches and pains, no matter how mundane. You have nothing to lose but a little face. But never take this Guardian/healer for granted. ASK him first! If you ask him, I can guarantee that he will respond, even if only to comfort you. No healer worth his salt can ever promise you a cure, and Cydwr is no exception to that ruling.

You do not have to *believe*, but it helps. You do not have to be a Christian, a Buddhist, a Muslim, a Jew or whatever. Just go with an enquiring mind, an open mind. It helps, too, if you have an open heart!

(Later on I checked the bridge by dowsing. It had a Courier line running almost parallel with it. Plus: a healing line that runs crosswise, about four feet wide. The other little bridge near the main A5025 had a healing line that just missed the bridge. I managed to move it directly over the flowing water. The bridge is now 'Healer Friendly', but lacks the rock formation, which generates greater energy. A Courier line is a Giver and Receiver of information connected to most Standing Stones by a seven looped spiral and in turn connected to EVERY human being on this planet by their chakric system.)

NOTE: *First published by One Vision.*

THE BOSHAM STONE

I was already aware about the whirling vortex of energy that Hanne Jahr had found in the grounds of *Bosham House*, covered in weeds and ancient roots. Her sensitivity had led her to the spot and she had spent many an hour in quiet meditation there 'knowing', with that inner voice that can thunder through one, that *this was a special place*: a Place of Power. But what it was she didn't know. What she *did* know, was that there was a special being connected with the site, a being that was multidimensional. But that was all.

During a question and answer session that she attended weekly, Hanne found out that the spot was an interdimensional *Gateway* of *Grail Energy* that had been capped. There were beings waiting to communicate from a higher level, to release once again the old esoteric knowledge that had been withheld from man/womankind for thousands of years for fear of misuse by the negative forces.

I was invited to come to *Bosham House* to witness this power/energy for myself, and, if possible, to invite this Angelic Force (for that is what it was) to use me to *uncap* this energy and release it from its bonds. I should point out that *anybody* could do this work either by prayer, meditation or visualisation, and that I was not something special. But the work *had* to be done by Man, had to have the *intent* of Man/Womankind. That was very important.

We sat around the power spot. I could feel the energy whirling in a clock-wise direction. I closed my eyes and waited. The channelling energy was not strong. I expected something to happen right away. But it didn't. We had to wait. The energy was gentle. Eventually a being spoke, an angelic being called *Seriph*, He told us that this Place of Power had been capped three thousand years ago. Using my arms and hands this gentle being began intricate passes and motions, sometimes fast, sometimes slow. He spoke as he worked explaining what he was doing and how it was necessary for a piece of granite to be placed on the site. The granite would amplify and refine the vortex, making communication easier. After five minutes or so it was done. He blessed us, and left as gently as he had arrived. Before we had started the energy field across the 'spot' had been about twelve feet across. Now it was three times that, and already on its way to the road and beyond. Seriph also told us that a *healing line* had been opened up which ran right through the vortex. He had pointed to a spot to his right and said that this was the main *healing point*, and that a permanent seat must be placed there. Hanne said that the spot indicated was the very spot where she had been inspired to sit all these months! Hanne dowsed for the healing line. She found it. I needed no more proof that this. This was indeed a special place. David Russell, the well-respected dowser and archaeologist, responded to my request for more information on this Power Site. I asked him to see, using his sensitive skills, whether a standing stone had been placed on this sacred site. My inner vision told me that it had! But I wasn't telling David that, anyway, I could be wrong. David rang back a couple of hours later. Not only could he confirm my vision but also the stone was still within a two and half-mile radius of Bosham and had been broken up as an aggregate!

By further dowsing I found out that the piece of granite needed was to be four and half foot tall and between twelve and eighteen inches across. A piece that size would cost £390 plus VAT! Inspiration struck: Pete and Jude Stammers lived a stones chuck from the *Avebury Stones* and these *sarson stones* were to be found in fields around their house in *West Kennet*. I phoned Jude and explained the position. She phoned back the next day to say that she had *found the Bosham Stone*!

Our next problem was raising the £235 needed to carry the Bosham Stone for the 300 mile round trip. With pledges from my two Earth Healing groups, plus the 'Friends of Bosham House', we not only raised the cash but what was left over paid for the special Healing Seat that Seriph had indicated.

On the 7th of November 1996 (7 being the number of *change*) the Bosham Stone came home. It went so smoothly that everybody held their breath waiting for something to go wrong. So here it was, the long awaited stone that was to become a focus for so many people over the years,and I 'knew' that it would also change the lives of many with its information and healing energy. The stone slipped into its hole as if climbing back where once it had stood thousands of years before. Thomas Hamblin would surely approve.

I will never forget Hanne's excited voice on the phone: "It's arrived and it's so beautiful, so beautiful." These words were all I needed to tell me that all the threads had pulled together to make a perfect whole, that our Bosham Stone had not only journeyed from Wiltshire but was once rolled and shaped under the vast shifting mass of the last ice age. A true granite Sarsen stone.

On Sunday 10th November I arrived at Bosham House. I beebed the horn and Steffie Sorrell appeared and waved me on toward the site of the stone. As I pulled round the old printing sheds and offices, I caught my first glimpse. It was as if the stone had always been there. As I pulled up a robin had settled on the stone. Steffie also saw this, and commented. It reminded us of the robin that came and sat on the typewriter of the poet and mystic Derek Neville one early morning and sang its heart out. Derek was a close friend of Thomas Hamblin.

As Hanne, Steffie and I sat on the newly acquired 'Healing Seat' (placed exactly where the angelic being had indicated), Steffie saw, with her inner vision, a golden bird settle on the stone. Later, driving back, I suddenly 'knew' what that symbolism meant. The golden bird represented the golden light of the Cosmic Christ, that descended on Jesus in the form of a dove, when he was baptised by John, when Jesus was first touched by the Christ Consciousness prior to his ministry. The Bosham Stone did not resist, as Jesus did not resist, receiving this baptism of gold, releasing the ancient wisdom back into the earth and all its peoples: radiating peace, love and truth. The Golden Heart that beats at the centre of all the true religions of the world. The Bosham Stone had come home.

NOTE: *First published by New Vision.*

"I understood with unequalled clarity what he was explaining. I didn't have to ask him for clarifications. My keenness of thought should have surprised me, but it didn't at all. I knew at that moment that I had always been crystal clear, merely playing dumb for someone else's benefit." DON JUAN MATUS.

PLAYING DUMB.

Sometimes when someone speaks, though it doesn't
    Always have to be
A powerful speaker, a speaker of substance, but a
    Whispered truth, an
Unconscious truth, uttered in the heat of the moment,
    Even the speaker does not
Always *know* that he speaks a truism. Yet it explodes
    Upon the mind and spirit
And thunders its way to the core of your being as if
    You have *always known this*
Truth, always known what it *was* and *is*. Something
    Opens in you and you are at
Once set free. And then gradually you forget again.
    The shutters go up, the
Fetters once again, are in place.
    It can be a piece of music, a poem, a love-
Song, or a bird singing whose
Beauty brings you within striking distance again,
    Even the sound of an axe

Chopping wood, the touch of a lover; and then you
    Forget; yes, always this forgetting
Remembering and forgetting again.
    Why is it that we forget so easily?
Let me tell you a story: *"There was once a man with*
*   a Wife and family. He, like his*
Father before him, and HIS father before that, led a
*   Seemingly blameless life. He*
Was a churchgoer and everything revolved around
*   The church. He beat his*
Children if they stepped out of line and beat his wife
*   If, she too, stepped out of*
True, and could see nothing wrong in that. He was a
*   Strict father and husband.*
*   When he wanted sex he took it, whether his*
*   Wife wanted it or not, that was*
His right. When he wanted a drink down the pub and
*   Came home drunk and beat*
The wife and kids, that was his right also. And when
*   He thought that he had gone*
Too far he would go to confession, just like his father
*   Before him, and be absolved*
Of his sins...until the next time. He worked hard, very
*   Hard, and brought his son*
Up to follow in his footsteps and the daughter to
*   Follow in his wife's footsteps."*
    And so the pattern developed, life after life.
The scenery would change,

The backdrop would change, but not the substance
Of his life. The woman, too,
Remained subservient in her attitude. That also went
On life after life.
When you are born you don't bring with you a
Personal spiritual *shopping*
List! You don't bring with you a questionnaire with all
The answers about what you
Should do and how to behave, do you? You leave
That up to your peers and
Religion. And rightly so! For are not your peers the
One's to go to for advice, is not
The church a teacher of moral code? But that
Depends on who your peers are,
That depends on how your particular religion
Interprets their particular teachings!
But then something happens that you *know* is
Outside of what your peers
Are telling you! *Outside* of what your religion is
Teaching you. You just KNOW
That it isn't true. Something bursts within you and
You become an *outsider*,
Questioning all the time about *chapter and verse.*
You question whether
The God of your religion is a gentle and loving God,
Or a warmonger, whether your
God is a moral God or an immoral God and whether
Your God is *in* everything

Or not? After all, God is supposed to have made
    Everything, created everything.
It's not that you *doubt* the existence of God. No, it's
    Not that. But is the creator
Without or within, or *both?!* Is your God a loving God
    Or a vengeful one? Or do
You, personally, have to find out?
    A person could have spent his whole life in a
    Little village far from
Anywhere of importance, he does not go to church,
    Does not follow any particular
Philosophy and yet has more wisdom in his little
    Finger then you could gain in
A lifetime, no THREE lifetimes! And his secret? It's
    No secret. He is *KIND* and
LOVING, as was his father before him and *his* father
    Before that. They brought
Their children up on *LOVE AND KINDNESS*.
    Wisdom grew in them without
Effort. That's not to say that sometimes one would go
    Astray, a runt in the litter but they would love it
    Just the same. On the whole they would
    Survive. They would automatically appreciate
All that *nature* would provide and in their *loving* and
    Kindness would grow wisdom.
Again, the crops may fail and they would have a bad
    Harvest. But they would

Shrug their shoulders and say: *that's the way of*
Things.
But that's not the way of it, is it? Those people
Are hard to find. Or are
They? Listen to the wind sometimes, or just listen to
Your heart, they will resonate
All that I have said and more. When in the quiet of
Your room and the quiet
Of your heart, *listen.* And if you are lucky Love will
Come roaring over the plain like
A wind, or sing to you amidst the presence of your
Heart, and your heart will
Swell with compassion for *all things* and leave you
With A peace that is beyond
Reason.
So next time your neighbour, or whoever,
Says something that
Breaks you open with *truth* and *joy,* that hits you like
A hammer...*tell* them, for
God's sake, TELL THEM, don't *'play dumb'.* And
When a song or poem, or the
Sound of a bird echoes amidst the peace of the
Forest and brings you to
Overflowing and tears course down your
Cheeks...shout for joy and LIVE in *that*
Moment. But above all, *REMEMBER.*

THE ALLOTMENT

Ben was the first, the biggest and the lustiest, already bawling for the breast. Gus was born several minutes later, small and blue, his cry a weak wheeze, his legs twisted and deformed as if still curled up in the womb. Three weeks later their mother died from a massive haemorrhage.

The twins' father left the early rearing of his twin boys to his elder sister, who had lost her husband to the sea and rejoiced at the opportunity to be a mother to her brothers' sons: to share her maternal love, to become at last *important* as a caring, though childless herself, member of the little fishing community where children were such a blessing.

Little Ben turned out to be sturdy, strong and inquisitive. He persistently asked questions till his father and aunt reeled with the onslaught. Whatever toys his father could afford to buy were systematically taken apart to see how they worked and methodically put back together again. He was a bonny lad, freckled and charming, loved by all. His quest for knowledge was unquenchable and at school he was without doubt the star pupil. Even at sport he excelled. He was everybody's favourite, everyone's champion. He had three failings, however, that would hound him all his life – *impatience, boredom* and the inability to *listen*. He always assumed that his natural ability to learn easily would hold him in good stead, that if he skipped a detail or two in whatever subject that he was studying it wouldn't matter because he could always go back to it later – but he never did. He became bored very easily, but his charm, personality, and wit were such that these few, small points were overlooked by his family and friends.

Gus held on to life like a feather caught in a tree, any minute a small gust of wind could wrench him back whence he came. But even with his obvious deformity and breathing difficulties his spirit was strong. His determination to hold on to life blazed throughout his little body. He was seven before he could walk. Even then, with the aid of callipers he could barely drag his legs, but he improved as the years passed, growing steadily in the shadow of his twin brother, whom he adored.

Gus's single most talent was his *patience* and his ability to find joy in small things. He *drew* exquisitely and, when his chest would allow him, sang more sweetly than any girl. His greatest joy was to ride in his father's wheelbarrow to the allotment. The allotment was situated in a small valley at the back of the village, protected by the, sometimes, fierce sea winds. The soil there was rich and vital, fed by dried seaweed and fishmeal. To Gus the allotment was the single most beautiful place in all the world. It was only there that he felt whole, only here where life was vibrant and energy fed him. But above all, there was peace – a peace so profound that he could not describe it, only in song. For it was here, and only here, that he sang, and his voice carried up and out of the little valley down into the village, and all who heard it would stop mending their nets; stop kneading dough; stop whatever they were doing, and listen entranced – captivated by the shear beauty of his song.

As the boys grew to manhood their own individual ways matured also. Ben became a fisherman like his father, for he loved the sea, but his restless nature and thirst for knowledge led him away from the quiet village community that he had always known. He joined a fleet of merchant ships travelling to and from Europe and beyond. He studied, and in time, received his *Master's Ticket*. Now he had his own ship to command and wherever his company sent him he always delivered on time.

He was a good master, and well respected. If the men had a problem they would always find him wise and sympathetic, and in a few years he was able to lease his own vessel, then another, and another.

By the time he was thirty he was a rich man. Everything a man could want was his. Women especially, were brought under his spell without any effort on his part. He owned property in London and in Spain. He ate only the finest food and drank wine that he himself imported from France. He was invited to only the best social functions and nine times out of ten was the guest of honour, for his wit and style were well known, and his generosity a legend.

During his ten-year absence from his home village he went back only once. Nothing had changed, and after a night or two with his family he was off again.

The restlessness in Ben persisted. All that he had, all that he owned, meant *nothing* to him. His inner self cried out for recognition. It was through this restlessness of spirit that Ben started his journey round the world.

Wherever he went he would seek out a spiritual master from whom he might learn the *ultimate wisdom*, and, as was his nature, when he grew bored, he used his charm to bluff his way through the more difficult studies and practices, fooling nobody but himself, thinking that his teachers would not notice. His teachers merely smiled a wry, secret smile.

He learnt many things, however – how to absorb liquid into his body merely by placing his hand into a bowl of water; how to levitate himself three feet off of the ground; how to generate heat from his body that would melt the snow around him as he meditated naked.

But these were merely yogic techniques. They did not satisfy him. He studied long and hard about the aspects and principles of the Godhead. He was intelligent. He *knew* that the God he sought lay *within*.

At how many feet of how many masters had he sat, each telling him to look *within*? Well, he'd tried looking within. He'd tried every technique of meditation and contemplation that he could find, but always there was something missing. He was a proud man and not used to failure, so he started to tell tales of his adventures with the wise men and ascetics that he had met on his travels, and he would demonstrate his yogic techniques of levitation and water absorption, and people were amazed at his skill and heaped praise on him.

But he was not satisfied – the inner longing persisted. Then he was introduced to *opium*. Some masters, he was told, used opium to induce visions. At first he took small quantities at regular times of the week. The opium indeed created visions within that thrilled him more than anything he'd known. The smoke was sweet and intoxicating. He journeyed far into the mind. At first, these regular journeys into the mind were controllable and satisfying. A strange bliss would settle on him as he inhaled the smoke from the pipe. But, as is the way of things, as time went on, to enable him to reach this state of bliss, he needed more and more opium. He was spending day after day smoking. He cared little for food or wine now. He smoked alone, his supply of opium being delivered to his place of residence. He grew thin, and his fine body wasted. He no longer needed people. Even women he shunned. Many tried to help him, but it was useless.

When he first began to smoke the drug he had a vision, the vision was of the old allotment, his brother Gus was seated in the old wheelbarrow...and he heard his song. The song that Gus sang was more beautiful than anything that he had ever heard, and he cried bittersweet tears. He never saw that particular vision again. He searched for it, oh how he searched for it, but no amount of opium brought it back.

It was at this stage that a master appeared. Not a drug induced master but a master under whom he had once been taught. He spoke kindly to his long-lost pupil, pointing out that he was now a *slave* to the substance, but a substance that could be defeated with little pain of withdrawal. Ben *knew* that he was sick; he knew that he needed help and was glad and full of love to see his old teacher reaching out to him. The master taught Ben powerful mantras, the sound of which vibrated throughout his whole body. The pain of withdrawal subsided. He swung the mantras inside him for many weeks, the master gently feeding him a little more food each day. The master slept by his side, never leaving him, until at last the beautiful mantra released him from his bondage. It was then the master, quietly and without ceremony, left him, knowing that he would never walk that particular path again. How the master became aware that Ben needed help he never knew, for he had betrayed this master, and many others, and now he felt shame, shame that in his deception a master *still* came for him, came to ease his pain. Ben had *never* acknowledged the secret smile that the masters and teachers that he had known, shared. Ben never forgot the master's kindness.

But it made little difference to his way of life; he again lived it to the full. And still he searched for the one thing that eluded him: inner *happiness* and *fulfilment*.

Gus often thought of his beloved brother, Ben, and when on that day years before, when Ben had come home to them, he rejoiced and wept with joy. New strength seemed for a moment to pour into his withered legs as he staggered toward him. Ben caught him before he fell, and held him close. Ben stayed for a night and a day, but seemed somehow pre-occupied. He seemed not to see his family, only to tolerate them, yet Gus *knew* that he loved them, loved his father, his aunt, loved *him*, but refused to show it – refused to acknowledge for reasons locked deep within him. Gus took Ben to the allotment to show him a new gardening technique that he had acquired and perfected. Eagerly he told Ben that each vegetable had its own character, that it grew better if planted next to a vegetable with whom it could respond, with whom it felt comfortable, just as people of a similar type are attracted to each other, and in so doing they flourish. Ben nodded his head. He only half listened. He got abruptly, hugged his brother, mumbled his goodbyes and was gone.

Gus sent a song after him to bring him back. The song surged pure and sweet, tugging at the striding figure of Ben as he climbed out of the valley, tears fell from his eyes in huge drops, but he did not stop, he had to get away.

Gus *knew* the struggle that continued to rage within his beloved brother, but he knew also that Ben would return, for he would run out of places to hide, though he could not hide from himself, yet hiding was what he was good at...or so he thought.

Years passed, and the brothers' father died leaving just the elderly aunt to look after Gus. Gus spent most of his time hobbling around the allotment, spending more and more time alone with his plants. The more he sang of the harmony he felt, the more the allotment flourished. He learnt about the healing power of herbs and plants and cultivated these precious simples alongside his vegetables. Folk would come to him from far and wide to consult him. Whence his knowledge came none ever knew, for they never questioned his ability and skill. Not only did he dispense herbs but people came to him for council, for he became wise in the ways of man and womankind, bringing happiness to a family that turned against itself, gently showing them how to restore their balance. Even the so-called insane were brought to him, and he sang to them and his song was so sweet that the inner pain of these poor souls was swept away, and even though the words he sang for them none could understand. Those who were more enlightened saw a light around Gus that they saw around no other.

Gus began to sleep in the small shed that his father had built on the allotment, for it became harder and harder for him to climb in and out of the valley. He never went hungry, those he helped paid him in fish and bread, and milk was brought to him daily. There were those who called him a saint or holy man, yet he never mentioned God or a supreme teacher; there were those that called him doctor, yet he had no training: he claimed that the plants communicated with him, telling him their secrets; there were those who worshiped his songs, yet even he did not know whence they came. Gus only knew *joy*, but pain also was a constant companion.

Ben at last saw the lights of home, his village way up on the cliffs. From there he could look down into the allotment valley. It was dark after a hot day in autumn and a mist had formed, its fingers stretching out in all directions, growing like fermenting yeast. For a moment he thought he could see a light down in the allotment valley, but how could that be? No one could tend his garden so near to darkness. He rubbed his eyes and looked again, 'yes' there *was* a light. It remained fixed as the mist swirled about it. Ben took the old path down and into the valley, stepping gently and carefully between each gardeners' patch. He made his way toward the light. As he approached, he heard the voice of his twin brother – it was the most compelling sound that he had ever heard, a song that saturated his spirit, spilling over and entering his heart: *it was a song of welcome!*

Ben's shoulders straightened as he opened the door to the little hut, as he opened the door the song stopped, and without looking up Gus said, "Hullo Ben, my dear brother, I was expecting you."

Gus was sitting in an old rocking chair, in front of him glowed an old oil lamp. The lamplight reflected in his eyes a fathomless quality of gentleness. Without getting up he opened his arms to his brother who knelt before him. They hugged each other for a long time. Finally Ben spoke:
"How did you know I was coming?"
"Oh, I just *knew*," replied Gus, "I just knew."
Ben told his brother that he never expected to return home again, never expected to see the village again.

The twins were fifty years old now, their father and aunt both now dead. Ben was tall and fine looking, his voice cultivated and commanding, his clothes the finest money could buy, but his eyes gave him away. They were dead, reflecting only disappointment and sadness.

Gus wore only the simplest of clothes. He had grown grey, and his legs were weaker, not having grown stronger to match his bodily growth. Occasionally he would grimace as he moved his limbs – but those eyes, those eyes: they glowed like rubies. To look into them was to touch the untouchable.

As Ben gazed at his brother, Gus again began to sing, and as he sang Ben began to see the whole of his life stretched out before him; the first journey out of the village; his first trip abroad; his rise to riches and fame. Ben was not aware that Gus was singing his life for him, for what he saw was so *real!* Gus's song curved high and then low, painting vivid pictures in the air. Ben saw himself at the feet of many masters; he saw their wry smile when he tried to cheat them; he saw again the wonder on the faces of his followers as he performed his yogic feats; he again felt the elation of the praise heaped upon him; felt the sadness of his defeat; the shame of his deceit, for never once did he find the God within. Then, like a revelation, he saw in a blaze of light his brother Gus, no longer crippled, no longer deformed but straight and firm and...and *next* to him was someone he barely recognised. For what seemed to him a small eternity he stared at the figure next to his brother for it was someone he dimly remembered...it was, no it couldn't be, it was... *himself!* And as he continued to watch, he saw Gus merge with this figure of himself. It was *then* that he *knew*, it was then that the spirit within leapt with joy and recognition, as light poured into his consciousness. Ben knew now that he and Gus were *one soul*, but that their minds had been split. He knew with clarity that it didn't matter that he had journeyed and learned so little for that was *his* choice, *his* journey. The flute players' call in the forest comes from *all* directions and he had *chosen* his path.

Gus, on the other hand, had little choice, seemingly. Ben had travelled the world seeing and experiencing many wonderful and extraordinary things. Gus had never moved from the village where he was born, yet his wisdom was a revelation.

As suddenly as the song started, it finished. Ben gazed at his brother. "I have been so foolish," he said. "I have experienced and seen many things in the world, yet I have seen *nothing*. I have seen you Gus, as you really are, as you have always been, but I never possessed the eyes to *see* until now," he bowed his head, "I am so ashamed."

Gus was silent. "Ben," he said quietly, "I too am ashamed," Ben looked up, surprised, " "But why...?" he said. Gus motioned him into silence, "you see, as a boy I worshipped you; I envied your skill at learning; your skill at athletics; your extraordinary curiosity and thirst for knowledge. And when you left I was consumed with envy, I too wished to travel your path, but just as you flung yourself headlong into your life, almost as if you were commanded to, I too flung myself into what I knew: I learned to listen to our father and came to realise how wise he was; how extensive his knowledge of the sea and the earth; I learned to love his physical strength as he lifted me into the old wheelbarrow and brought me up here; I listened to him tell how he used to speak to his small family of plants; I also listened to him singing to himself, oh so quietly."

"I never heard him sing," said Ben, surprised.

"No, you would not have done. He sang only for me, and his plants. It was from him that I learned to *really* sing; from him that I learned the power of stillness; from him I learned of the cathedral *within*. If it had not been for our father, who only taught those who were willing to listen, my envy of you would have turned to jealousy, which in turn may have turned to hate. Instead my love for you grew...and now it overflows. You have come home, not just in the bodily sense but home in the inner realm, now you are in touch with your *real* self for the first time. You now have your ears and heart open, and, if you wish it, I will teach you all I know, for there are so many who are in need and the joy they bring cannot be measured."

Ben sat and thought for a very long time. Finally he looked up. "I have travelled the whole world searching for something, or maybe trying to escape. I forgot that wherever I went I would carry myself with me. I ignored the wry smiles of the holy men when I attempted to cheat them with my intellect. I was cheating only myself. When I left so abruptly after my visit all those years ago, it was because I recognised in *you* all that I craved but would not accept: that you had *found* what I was looking for, sitting in the middle of *this* allotment. I envied you just as you envied me, and I could see how destructive that emotion was. So I got up and left. But when you sent after me the song to bring me back, I had to use all my strength of will to resist, and I having been resisting ever since. That song haunted my dreams; that song invaded my silence; that song was the most powerful thing I have ever heard...and I could resist no longer. But you will have no need ever to sing it again, for I have truly *come home*! I shall labour for you, fetch for you, and even carry you, should the need arise, but above all I shall listen, *really* listen, perhaps for the first time in my life, and *learn*."

Gus began to sing, his voice carried out of the little hut, out of the valley and down to the village, he sang in a sweet, strange language known only to him, for those who were asleep, it mingled with their dreams and for those who were awake, they knew that Ben had returned – this time to stay!

NOTE: *First published by The Quarterly.*

THE SEEDS
(1993)

The cosmic masters, under the influence of the Universal Mind, came together for council: something *had* to be done

After the collapse of the continents of Mu, Lemuria and finally Atlantis, they knew that it was only a matter of time before mankind again created weapons of mass destruction. They knew also that the *next* time the WHOLE of the Earth would be contaminated, and not just by industrial poisons, not by man-made disease, but by the introduction of negative beings that were just biding their time before incarnating once again for the purpose of self-gratification and worship of the lower Self. Yes, something *had* to be done!.

After much soul-searching, the masters came up with the *only* solution: if negative beings were set to incarnate and bring havoc to the great Earth Goddess then they too must prepare advanced souls with the job of raising the consciousness of human beings, steering them back on course for the incredible journey back to the source, to merge and become One with all things, bringing back all that they had experienced to the Eternal, for that was the supreme *idea* of the Infinite in the first place.

The only weapon, however, that they would be permitted to use was *'Love'*, the ability to love the Divine Fire that burned in *all* beings, no matter how corrupt or imbalanced they may have become.

Word was sent out to the many universes, that the Holy of Holies had created, for volunteers who would enter a training program for the great dawning of the Aquarian Age, a time of immense, spiritual change, but also a time when the dark ones, the negative ones, would do all in their power to prevent the spiritual change that the planet *had* to undergo.

The planet itself, like the human beings on its surface, HAD to undergo change. For nothing stands still, all is transient, all is life and must ultimately claw its way back to the divine source, no matter what form or shape it might take on. All are in the mind of the Eternal, and the essence of the Eternal is composed of Love, a Love that reproduces itself, because its very nature is to BE and to CREATE, to share this wonderful power called Love.

Word was sent out, and millions responded to the call. Many were called though few were chosen; those that *were* chosen were called *'The Seeds'*, for within them lay such Love that it lit up the whole of the cosmos. But they were warned that further incarnation on Earth, where they would be exposed to all the lower desires of the third dimension, could well result in a lessening of the flame within them.

They, like most human beings, would begin to suffer from spiritual amnesia: a forgetting of 'who they truly were, where they had come from, and what their purpose on Earth was. Ultimately, their job was to help their fellow human beings (though some were not of human form but were to incarnate *into* a human body) to attain some semblance of Cosmic Consciousness.

The great spiritual masters told this army of the light of the suffering they must undergo, in their struggle to regain the knowledge of 'who they really were', and what their assignment was.

To help them, extraordinary symbols were to be created, vast mandalas of light. Each soul would respond to his or her symbol. Many would *share* a symbol, for these patterns were universal, used on *other* planets, other vibrations of creation.

When the time came the forces of nature, under the loving gaze of the Earth Goddess, would be summoned. These very symbols would be etched into the living corn of the planet, and the curious would queue up to view them. They would be photographed and broadcast throughout the world, their beauty admired by millions. There would be those who would ridicule and scoff. There would be those who would imitate these cosmic works of art;

but not before the 'Seed Memory' is stimulated, not before the Seed cracks and begins to open and memory begins to stir.

And when society becomes bored with these patterns then will appear sacred symbols etched in 'light': great swirling bands of glorious illumination that will fill the skies all over the Earth. Millions more will begin to remember.

Also at this time the greater and lesser religions of the Earth will rise up and accuse the Seeds of evil doings, for the Seeds will speak of the One-In-One who embraces ALL religions, even those who worship the great places of power, dotted throughout the landscape, where the balance of nature, though greatly disturbed, is adored.

The channelling of information from spiritual entities far out in the cosmos, yet perhaps only a micro-second away, will communicate, offer teachings through human beings so gifted in this art. But all must be aware of deception...for it will come. New books will be written, for the sacred books, the holy books of the great world religions have been tampered with, though great teachings and truths still remain, though heavily edited, down through the ages. Poets and musicians will begin to tell *their* stories, for the Seeds work through *all* creative gifts.

So then do the *Dark* ones. But beauty will dispel the shadows: light and truth will once more permeate the Earth, raising her to a new frequency of understanding, one step nearer to the source.

True Love cannot be disguised its power never measured. The time is NOW! Nothing can stop it; it is as if it is already done: on a higher level it already *is*.

The view of this planet from space is so familiar to us now; this beautiful blue planet swathed in misty, swirling clouds of vapour, set in a backdrop of a diamond studded void. But, using clairvoyant sight, the view is very, very different: from the surface of the Earth radiates a rainbow of colour, a spectrum that makes the *normal* sight of the Earth pale into nothingness, a sight so rare and beautiful, so harmonious that one weeps at the wonder of it. These colours correspond with out own human aura: a reflection of our physical, mental and spiritual state.

But that is NOT the way it is now:

The colours are now muddy, shuddering bands of contaminated energy, the bright lines of power, the etheric grid of the planet, now lay twisted, broken and blocked. The Great Mother is in pain. She needs to move, to adjust Herself ready for this great influx of spiritual change.

Supreme beings form the 5th dimension draw close, ready to pour energy and light into the Earth. Already they are making adjustments to the planets, speeding up the frequency rate of all physical matter. Even now time is speeding up. Haven't you noticed? Even though the planet appears to revolve at its accustomed rate?

But these great beings cannot bring the changes without *our* help, without YOUR help. Light and change can only be brought to the Earth and anchored here by human beings! The golden light of the Christ continually pours down upon the Earth, but it must be received and 'earthed' by US, the human race! The Christ consciousness is pre-CHRISTIAN, the Christ consciousness is pre-EARTH, the Christ consciousness is *God made manifest*!

The Dark ones will fight for supremacy, fight for what they believe is theirs, forgetting that all belongs to the One. But they will lose, for the light is supreme and even *they* will mend their errors for no one is lost, *no one*. The light will gather even *them* up in its arms and take these loved ones to itself: For the light is All, the light is LOVE.

The seeds came thick and fast now: beautiful, bright, pulsating spheres. They flowed like a huge river from the 'Cathedral of Light' that

belonged nowhere, yet was everywhere. They cascaded out, filling the dark void that was a universe, blown from the source, the Place of Light, seemingly seconds before.

As they drew further away from the light each sphere separated and became two, a duality flying side by side, though they were ALWAYS aware that they were One.

The Place of Light receded, and from its vast interior came a sound, music so joyous that it was as if this 'song' was a mighty horn heralding the coming of a great army of creative beings. The sound followed the spheres out into the limitless immensity of space, sang to them as a mother sings to her children, and they knew bliss. The sound they heard was the great AUM!

NOTE: *First published by SC Magazine.*

THE STOOPING GODDESS
(Archetypes)

Dictionary definition of 'archetype' is (1) an original pattern or model; a prototype. (2) A transcendent entity of which existing things are imperfect realisations. A simplistic way of explaining would be mould taken from the original, perfect in every way. What was it that a certain master said: 'By their fruits shall you know them'.

Let me start by describing *my* personal archetype of the Earth Goddess Ayesha (or Gaia, or Diana. She has many names). I 'see' her as a voluptuous Greek beauty, curvaceous and distinctly sexy in her flowing garments and tied-up hair. I see her as the earth itself: fertile and beautiful, yet firm and strong, putting up with no nonsense, on the other hand, vulnerable and open. That's *my* vision of her. There are those of you whose view is entirely different, showing her as a vast energy field of indescribable colours that go right off the spectrum, or as a spiral, whirling and shimmering with immense power. But I'll come back to The Goddess later.

Whether you be a Christian, Buddhist, Sikh, Muslim, Hindu, Pagan, or whatever, your belief structure, you will have your ideal archetype. It may be Jesus 'The Christ', crucified on the cross of Injustice; the golden Buddha sitting on the lotus flower of enlightenment; the Pagan with their vision of Pan, god of animal, vegetable, and mineral, with his pipes held to his lips whilst skipping merrily on golden hooves. Or like the Indian deity Shiva, dancing out the universe, one foot set firmly on earth. Whatever supernatural healing takes place you will attribute that healing to either one of these and more; whatever miracle you experience, what ever your saving grace. The Great Spirit of the Red Man, represented on their totems (the Australian aborigine, also) as the very animals and birds that they see running free in the *every day* of their lives, runs equally free in *them*. These are their archetypes. Whether or not you have an enlightening experience, one that you would term *mystical*, or a religious experience, wanting to shout it from the rooftops, tell everyone, make them listen. You can bet that nine-times-out-of-ten you experienced it *on your own*, whether you employed an archetype or not, *that experience is real* and came from *within*. Not anyone else's experience, but *yours*. Whether you allow it to change your life, or make necessary adjustments to it, is up to you. But deny it at your peril. For as sure as god made little green peas and Birdseye, it will come round again. Trust me.

Each age has its heroes, its archetypes, and each age is *correct*. We all need to pin a name on something. A modern archetype, for example, is the *Statue of Liberty* representing *The Land of the Free*. Some may disagree with that, but you know what I'm saying.

A friend of mine, Malcolm Murduck, a sculptor, carved a modern representation of *The Green Man* for Leeds castle in Kent. A Pagan archetype, which, like Pan, represents all that is green and growing. When it was finally installed, Malcolm wept. Maybe he wept because his work had a kind of *finality* about it, to be seen by hoards of people down the centuries and become, possibly, *their* archetype by adoption. To be set in the concrete of their unconscious minds. Or maybe he wept just because he was proud that all his skill and energy had eventually paid off and hoped that his representation of this particular archetype would appeal to the masses.

Believe it or not but my own personal archetype (*one* of them, that is) for the sense of RETURNING HOME, is a Fish and Chip Shop! Why? Because I was brought up in a fish restaurant where all was cosy and warm, where my parents lived and all my brothers and sisters. It represented family and all that was *safe.* It usually appears when I am lost in the Dream State and all is dark about me. Then a light appears in the distance and I am drawn inexorably toward it. *Always* it is run by females: plump and motherly, full of smiles (The Goddess?).

The Infinite is a collective that does not have any truck with *time and space.* It sends us what we need at any particular time. Whether we have the sense to *know* it or *grab* it is another matter.

Why *The Stooping Goddess?* Lately, when I *see* a whirling vortex of energy that needs to be released (I know a lot of you are involved in this work) I see the Lady Ayesha, the Earth Mother, *stooping.* It's as though she has just walked into a room that has a very low ceiling. Then I know that she needs releasing in that spot so that she can stand upright again. As I may have described in other articles: vortexes all over the planet have to be made free for the esoteric knowledge to be released again, the *plug* or *seal* was set by 'angelic forces' to prevent *negative* intelligence's from grabbing it and plundering its secrets. The world has no need for them any more. The worst is over. So angelic forces must remove them...but only through the agency of Human Beings! Human Beings *must* take the responsibility, must take this final leap in consciousness, or *faith* if you like.

Whilst I'm on the subject of angels: years ago, whilst in Paris, staying with a French family, I decided to drive into the centre of Paris to see the sightes. Jacque, the head of the family, raised his hands and rolled his eyes as only the French know how: "You are going to *drive* into Paris?" he said, his thick French accent going up a register. "Are you crazy? Are you insane? You will not be able to park *anywhere*! I 'ave seen people *stabbed* for za parking. You must take the Metro." He insisted. I had never seen Jacque so worked up. "You know the reasons why, Jacque," I said, "I cannot walk that distance, cannot manage the Metro." He gave a shrug and a last gesture of despair, (as only the French know how).

My mate John Webster and I set out for the centre of Paris. We parked *right outside* Notre Dame Cathedral. We parked *right outside* the Louvre. We parked *right outside* the Eiffel Tower and rounded the trip off with a restaurant of which we parked; you guessed it, *right outside*. Before setting out I had asked my parking angel to do its stuff. It rarely fails me.

One day, in Spain, we had left the coach for the day and went walkabout in this little Spanish seaside town. I had left the wheelchair behind and had to walk. We had lunch and promptly got lost. The coach left at 3pm. Suddenly a huge wind got up. So strong a wind was it that the cars were nearly lifted off the ground. I grabbed hold of some railings. Just up ahead was a turning. We headed one step at a time for the corner and were literally *blown* around it. There, in the distance, was the coach. Immediately the wind ceased as suddenly as it had begun. Coincidence? Or a simple *Cosco?* (Cosmic Coincidence)

NOTE: *I have had this vision for the last 30 years or so. The Earth Goddess, carved in stone, lies asleep on her side, hands pillowing her cheek. Her naked body lies in a stream somewhere, carved out of one of the natural stone steps. The water tumbles and flows over her body. I want to take her in my arms and, still dripping, kiss her gently awake (always the romantic in me), remove all traces of poison apple from her beautiful mouth, put the golden leaves of autumn back in her hair and let her run with the wind:* **Free at last! Free at last!**

THE OAK OF THE PLAIN

THE land was barren and had been for nearly a century. Bush and scrub were all that were left of a once proud and thriving community.

When the war came the men were ordered to fight for a country they knew nothing about; a country that, until that time, refused even to acknowledge that they existed, except to extract taxes from their meagre crops once a year. But they had been happy, content to work the land and raise children. Theirs was a peaceful community. Hunger they knew and accepted as part of their way of life.

They ate only what they grew and killed a goat or ox only to sustain their own lives when the crops failed. But that was long ago. And the men never returned from the slaughter of war and the women and children moved away to the towns and cities and were swallowed up in the raw confusion of town life. What trees were left on the now desolate plain died now as if in grief at the leaving of the humans that they had grown to love. As they died what water was left dried up, leaving the stinging wind to roar over the plain without restraint and little pity. No bird could survive, only the towering eagles with their rifle eyes and echoing cried.

THE young boy of barely seven years climbed the plain. The young boy with the liquid brown eyes that reflected eternity carried with him a canvas bag filled with damp moss and a stout staff. As he walked the grass around his feet seemed to shimmer as if bombarded by an invisible rain. The wind for once stopped its driving howl and seemed to whimper in delight at this vibrant stranger. As he approached the summit, the highest point of the gently sloping plain, the young boy looked around him and saw stretched in all directions nothing but sorrow where once there had been joy and wept as a child weeps at the death of a beloved pet, for he knew compassion as an old friend, and although young in years the boy had a mission, one that would stretch far into time, one that would take his whole lifetime to accomplish.

With outstretched arms the boy seemed to embrace the land. A thrill vibrated through the ground where he stood and for a moment there was a profound silence and during that silence the boy drove his staff deep into the summit. Out of his bag of damp moss he took a single acorn . Then holding it aloft a great sound was heard, so strange and thrilling a sound that the invisible forces of nature seemed to leap in response. Then with much reverence he pulled the staff from the earth and dropped the acorn into the hole. The boy filled in the hole with some of the damp moss. He stood for a while looking down at this seemingly small deed, then with a last look he descended the plain and went back whence he came.

DURING that summer a small oak sapling appeared. Although the land was dry and rocky, apart from the odd patch of scrub grass, the sapling seemed to thrive as it grew, so too did it's awareness.   As the years passed, the tree grew steadily and after seven years could now be seen standing proudly at the summit on the plain. The young tree's consciousness expanded within it without effort. Although the wind tore at it the tree knew that it had to be so for it needed to grow in strength and the wind only could strengthen it. The grass around the tree seemed also to thrive for the young roots of the oak were drawing moisture up from the ground.

As the seventh summer came to a close a terrible longing overcame the young oak. Such a sense of expectation consumed him that he quivered in anticipation. Something was going to happen. But what? He did not understand.   Then   suddenly his senses, which could stretch as far as the eye could see, leapt with a great joy. For he could sense a presence. A huge light seemed to sweep the plain and again he quivered in all his branches. As the sun began to set a tall figure could be seen striding over the plain.

The young boy, now a youth, had returned. The young man with the liquid brown eyes that reflected eternity, shielded his eyes against the brilliance of the setting sun. And there waiting to greet him, silhouetted against the dying light, was the young oak tree, as strong and tall as the youth himself.. The youth quickened his pace and planting his staff firmly into the hill made his way quickly to the summit.

As the youth climbed a tranquil light seemed to dance over him and a strange, beautiful sound filled the air; a sound the young oak seemed to recognise but could not understand. The youth came within a few feet of the young oak; he stood quietly for a while, his beautiful eyes gleaming in the rays of the fading sun. Then he lifted his arms, walked forwards and embraced the young tree. The young oak tree had *never* known such joy. Who was this creature that he seemed to know so well? And a thrill again ran through him almost to a point of pain. The only creatures the young oak had ever seen were the eagles and their small prey, but this creature was different and he loved him beyond loving.

The youth sat with his back to the tree facing the setting sun and again the strange but beautiful sound filled the air and the young oak trembled with ecstasy. Soon the sound ceased and the youth dropped his head and slept. The oak stood guard over his new friend yet somehow he felt that he had always know him and always would.

That night the wind did not blow at all and the air was calm and warm. All the time that the body of the youth touched the young oak tree he felt more content and whole than he had ever been.

As the first rays of the sun spilt over the land the youth stirred. He stretched and then opening his pouch he took out bread and cheese and a container of water. Spreading the food on the ground, he blessed them, than ate and drank. The tree watched his friend and knew that he would not stay long and already felt sadness. Then he was aware that the youth was speaking to him.

"Seven years ago I planted you on this spot. I choose you from many hundreds of acorns because I *knew* that within you lay the essence of wisdom and strength and love. You have been chosen, as I have been chosen, to bring joy back to this desolate place. Your destiny is greater than you know, and your spirit is *my* spirit. For although you are and tree and I am a man, all life is one. I have brought with me this time a whole family for you to look after. For you are destined to be the centre of a great nation. When first I carried you to this summit, wrapped in damp moss, you were as asleep, but now you are awake. This time I have brought seeds. During the next seven days I shall plant them and you shall direct me as to where I sow – for you shall be the *Centre*."

The young oak thrilled with response to these beautiful words.

During the next seven days the youth directed by the young oak sowed the seeds of many, many trees. Before he planted he blessed each and every seed, and again the strange yet beautiful sound filled the air. Yet the sound came not from the youth but from the very air as if unseen forces were rejoicing in the planting of the seeds.

As the days passed the youth planted further and further away, yet to the young oak it was as if he never moved for his mind was linked with the mind of the youth and he *knew* that it would always be so.

When the planting was done the youth came once again to sleep his last sleep against the sturdy frame of his friend, the oak. But this time he was filled with sadness and tears ran down his cheeks, and the tree cried too for he felt at one with the youth.

The next morning the last of the bread and cheese was blessed and eaten. The youth stood back from the tree and spoke:

"Goodbye my friend, but fear not for I shall return. I am destined to do so for my whole life is dedicated to you and this seemingly desolate place, but you and I *know* of the beauty that lies hidden, and you and I will show it to those who understand. Our minds and spirits are one. Look over our new family and teach them well and talk to our friend, the wind, to be gentle with our children for they are not as strong as you."

The youth embraced the tree and once more the tree swelled with joy...and sadness.

WINTER came and went and the young oak now became aware of new life stirring beneath the earth. Small points of light grew steadily stronger as each seedling struggled upward. As they grew so their light and consciousness grew. By the end of the summer a haze of green could be seen growing in a perfect spiral that radiated out from the young oak standing proudly at the summit. The seedlings had been sown in such a way as not to crowd its neighbour when eventually reaching maturity.

The young oak felt a great sense of pride as he surveyed his growing family and the young saplings grew to love and revere their elder brother, the oak, who stood so tall and strong on the summit.

The young oak would tell the tale of the creature with the dark eyes who had planted him where he stood and of his great love for this man, and he would tell how he directed the youth to plant them where they now stood and not *one* of the seedlings had failed to grow. All, Without exception, were now part of the family of trees growing gently down to the plain. He told his eagerly listening family that after a few years their *own* seed would be blown by the wind to populate the vastness of the land and they would experience the joy of creation and the harmony that comes so easily to trees.

A further seven years passed and again the oak felt that terrible sense of expectation as though something were about to happen and he *knew* within himself that his friend, the man with the dark and beautiful eyes, was drawing near. All the trees around him began to quiver for they too felt something wonderful. Again the oak heard that strange and beautiful, mystical sound that that vibrated throughout the small woodland near the summit and once again saw the light that shimmered and glowed. Suddenly, there he was – the youth, now a man, was once again climbing the gently sloping hill and as he climbed he touched each and every tree that he had planted seven years before and as he touched them he blessed them and each tree felt such a power of love and wholeness that they cried out in silent ecstasy and joy. So this was the man that the oak spoke of with such love.

The man made his way up the spiralling family of trees, blessing as he went, until he stood once more in front of his friend, the oak. Then with tears in his beautiful eyes he embraced his old friend. The man spoke:

"We have both grown taller, my friend, but where I have stopped you will continue to grow taller and wider and your wisdom will become legend when our family eventually grows to maturity. You, my friend, will continue to teach the love that is at the centre of *all* things. For trees and plants understand with more ease the working of nature and harmony. As you continue to teach here I too continue to teach in my own land to my own kind. But they live in such confusion, they have so much pain in them and it is so hard to teach them to love. For my own kind do not love easily as you do. Learning how to love and live in harmony with their fellows can take many lifetimes."

The oak listened to his friend but not really understanding. Were not *all* men like his friend and why was it so hard to love and live in harmony? These things were natural for trees. The man spoke also of *hate* but the oak did not know what hate was except that it sounded an ugly word.

"My old friend, I have never spoken to you of hate for in nature it does not exist and there is no reason for you to know of it. I am part of you and you are part of me. We are *one* but only on the level of love. When I come to you I recharge this body, for only out here where there is no contamination from human thought can I regain my inner peace. If I were to teach of our love for one another I would be considered mad and all my teachings would fall and be trampled on. There are a chosen few of my kind who understand and one day I shall bring them to you for even *they* do not understand fully of what we *know*. When our family has grown and multiplied then I shall bring them to meet you and I shall take my rightful place beneath your branches and teach them of our love and the universal love that is *all things*."

When the man had finished speaking the oak again trembled in all its branches and joy filled the air and the young forest and basked in the pure light that radiated from the man. This then was the creature that the oak had spoken of so many, many times; this then was the man who blessed and planted them; and they rejoiced that he was at last amongst them and once again the strange and beautiful sound filled the air as if a hidden orchestra were playing; as if the seven kingdoms of nature were singing praises at the new life that had been planted, that they might again live in harmony fulfilling the role that they had been created for: harmonious growth and the ability to multiply.

AS the years passed this select family of threes, ask, elm, poplar, elder, and many, many more matured and grew more quickly than most for they had been especially blessed and charged with great power. Their elder brother, the oak, who stood on the summit, spoke often of the creature called man and how the man with the dark eyes was a part of him and was the sole reason for his enormous structure. For the oak had grown so very tall, for oaks usually take centuries to grow as tall as he and even longer to grow as wide. The oak spoke often to his family:

"You will all multiply and cover the vastness of the plain with your own kind and in time other creatures will come amongst us: creatures unlike the holy man who is our benefactor: creatures with *four* legs. Already water is springing forth from the ground as we continue to throw down our roots and drink. Already birds nest in our branches and reward us with their song; for they have a right to do so; it is the way of things."

Fourteen years passed and the plain was now thick with trees. Wild flowers from everywhere, and deer populated the forest that had grown up as if from nowhere, and there sitting proudly on the summit the great oak surveyed its ever-growing family and such happiness filled him as he had only experienced once before when the creature with the dark eyes embraced him and told him of his love.

A silvery stream now wove its laughing way through the forest and fish leapt with delight in the deep pools. Otters swam and fished and played leaving a spiral of crazy bubbles in their wake. The harmony created by the planting of one single acorn could not be measured, for such happiness was beyond reason. But the great oak, for all its wisdom, still yearned for the return of his friend.

THEN, as it had happened fourteen years before, a wonderful feeling of anticipation fell upon him and the oak quivered in all its branches: the immediate family of trees that the creature had blessed and planted *also* felt this strange yet wonderful quiver; they asked their elder brother, the oak, "What was this strange feeling?"

The oak answered: "He comes. The creature with the dark eyes, my soul brother, returns. What you feel is his presence for his presence walks *before* him and *behind* him in the same way that you, my family, radiate out from me."

A profound silence fell upon the forest and a warm breeze filled with the scent of a thousand wild flowers filled the air. Not a sound could be heard. Even the stream lowered its voice. A fantastic light permeated the forest and then like an echo of long ago that strange yet beautiful sound filled the forest; such a sound that could almost be touched and yet was untouchable. It seemed to come fro the very air yet had no point of entry, no centre from which it emerged. The sound this time was greater and more perfect than ever it was on that single day so many years before when the boy with the dark eyes first set foot on the plain. And with the sound came a light. At first a faint and gentle glow like the fire in a hearth warming and lightening a darkened room – and like the sound the light came from within having no starting point. It seemed to envelope every leaf, every branch, every blade of grass, drawing out from them a blaze that did not begin but was *always* there, waiting for birth.

The great oak's spirit swelled up like a giant beacon. Light burst from its immensity like a million suns and as the light reached out it embraced an equal light that radiated up from the plain and that marvellous, holy sound in the forest was joined by an even greater shout as every animal, every bird, every insect, raised its voice in joy, for the man with the dark eyes had returned to the place of desolation that was desolate no more!

THE man whose eyes mirrored eternity embraced his old friend once again. This time they both *knew* that they had never been apart. Physical touch only heightened the great love that had grown in such splendour. The man rested his staff against the great oak at took his now accustomed place at the foot of his friend. For many days the man just sat and communed with his great family. The trees asked him many questions and each was answered without exception, but the answers seem to come from both, man and oak, as though they were one.

But when asked where the man had come from and where he went only the man answered for the oak did not know the ways of men, only that they were different, and he listened with great interest, as the man told of vast cities where human beings lived, of hate and deceit, anger and greed, also their wonderful gifts of creativity: the gifts of music, painting and building. He told of vast oceans where huge ships carried men and women from one land to another.

But the trees wanted only to know how man lived with man; how he thought; what he thought. Did man know of trees and what was pain? The man told of how his kind had lost teir way; that they did not know harmony and joy as trees did. He told of man's gift of *freewill* that he may do with life what he wills. The trees did not understand for they knew only that they lived and all around them lived, that they were part of a perfect system that had been created out of an *imperfect* system. They knew because the oak had told them of their beginning. The man told of his struggle to bring light and knowledge to his fellow man and how stubborn man was. With all his skill man was but a child compared with nature.

Deep within man was the natural resource of love and harmony but somewhere along the way he had became blind to it for there were seemingly greater things in the world than love: there was wealth and possession and the ability to dominate one another: there were pleasures of the senses sacrificed by the disintegration of their bodies: diseases came and went, as one was cured another took its place – for they had lost their way. Great men of light and wisdom who led nations spoke out with a loud voice that peace and the ability to love was the only way to harmony; but such men of light were cut down by the forces of darkness, the darkness of ignorance that continually waged war within each and every man. Man slaughtered each other for the sake of peace but they did not know what inner peace really was for such knowledge had been lost. The man with the dark eyes told of his struggle to teach in such a world. It was only his union with his soul mate, the oak, that kept him alive. It was that union and the union with the tree family that kept him from being swallowed up by his fellows. For his fellow man found it so hard to love someone who had wronged them; so hard to see that they were *all* men and *all* one, having the same thoughts and defects. They could only see themselves as a single unit and one that must dominate and conquer the other. To allow love to enter their lives was a sign of weakness and that would never do. If only they could become trees ... "If only they could join all of you here in this beautiful forest then maybe they would begin to understand."

The oak thought for a moment and then spoke to the man: "Could you not bring your fellows here that they might join us?"

The man shook his head: "The plain that is now a forest is sacred. Only I know where it lies. For unbeknown to you this forest, this family, has been chosen to retain its secret. For in reality you lie high up in a vast mountain range that man cannot reach. If man were to come here they would destroy you for that is their nature. Mankind knows only how to *take*, he has not learned to *give*. In time perhaps I shall bring a chosen few of my fellows but that time is not yet."

The man stayed far longer this time than ever before for his inner strength had taken a terrible beating from the dark forces. It was only here in this sacred forest that he could renew his strength and regain his sanity. He drank the cool clear waters of the stream and bathed his body in the deeper pools. The otters played with him, laughing at his clumsy efforts to swim with them. He ate the fruit that now grew in abundance, sharing cherries and plums with squirrel and bird. Oh how he longed to stay among the trees he loved, but he loved his fellow man equally and he knew he must return to sow more seeds of truth into mankind.

The forest and all that lived there loved the man who radiated so much joy but felt also his moments of despair when his beautiful dark eyes filled with tears and he would weep uncontrollably. His sadness would not last long but it left a strange feeling of emptiness that the oak and the forest had not known before. But soon that was forgotten as the musical laughter of the man with the dark eyes echoed throughout the forest and bird and animal alike responded to his joy. Birds would stand on his head and shoulders, deer and rabbit would eat from his hands, for they did not know fear and this man who gave so much love knew that, but he also knew that his kind would take advantage of their trust for the world of men was in such turmoil. Their values so different from that of the tree family.

Soon he bade farewell and taking up his staff he walked slowly and painfully down the gentle sloping plain. Although the light around him was bright and vibrant, recharged by his friends of the forest, there was a subtle, subtle change. He bent a little now, where before he was straight. It was as if he were preparing himself for a great weight to be lowered onto his shoulders and he walked in readiness.

The whole forest sang for him – every blade of grass, every leaf, every animal and bird – but also, when his light could no longer be seen, they wept, wept at his going, at his departure from them. The great oak feeling their despair spoke to them:

"The man with the dark eyes is my brother. We are one, and even though he has gone from us I remain with him always. For since his last visit he has shared many secrets, most of which I cannot reveal, but even though his light has gone he remains in me and *his* strength is *my* strength and I shall share it with you."

As the years passed the forest grew even more beautiful and plentiful. The stream became a river and fish leapt in silver splendour, whilst animals multiplied and were never hungry.

Many more years passed. Seasons came and went and the memory of the man became a legend for he planted the first tree, the great oak, that stood tallest and widest on the summit on the plain. For an oak to be so tall at 56 years was a miracle, but then he had been especially chosen by the man with the dark eyes to be the first on the plain. He was chosen to guide the man in the planting of the gigantic forest in its infancy. The seven kingdoms of nature had done the rest.

THIRTY-FIVE years had passed since the man had left the forest and only the oak knew of his progress amongst men. Only the oak knew of his courage and of his mammoth task to show men how to love, to show men what love was.

But suddenly the light in the great oak grew steadily dim and in the far distance a terrible roar was heard as if giant hands were tearing at the very fabric of the planet. Even the sun's light was lessoned and the perfect harmony of the forest jolted as if something had tipped the scales – something terrible. Darkness covered the forest and the trees asked the great oak what had befallen them, but the great oak did not know and he felt sadness and despair for the first time. Not the despair felt by the departure of his beloved brother but by a certain knowledge that his friend was in danger yet was getting closer to him and the forest he loved.

After many days the great rumbling that shook the very roots of the forest subsided. The river whose flow had lessoned ran with strength once more – and down on the furthest reaches of the plain where the forest ended could be seen small dots weaving their way toward the forest. These were not animals...but *men*!

The great oak spoke to his family: "My friends, the man with the dark eyes draws near. I know that he is sick in mind and body and will need all our strength to restore him. Many years ago my brother told me that one day he would bring others of his kind to our beautiful home. Well that time has come. The world as they knew it has been destroyed because man has abused the world more than the world could bear, but my brother, the man with the dark eyes, has brought the chosen few and they will dwell amongst us. Make them welcome, brothers and sisters of the forest, for they too are your brothers and sisters.

Forty to fifty men, women and children now made their way up through the forest. Some were black; others white; some were yellow; some were red; others were brown. There were those whose eyes were narrow; there were those whose eyes were round; but *all*, all of them, shone with the great light and wonderment of finding such a beautiful place, a place that was reflected in those eyes.

Lying on a stretcher, being carried by two men, lay the man with the dark eyes. His light had grown dim and his beard long and grey. His staff lay beside him as if to comfort him. Every now and then he would raise his arm to point the way. As he grew near to the summit he motioned his bearers to put him down and with their help they raised him to his feet. Taking up his staff he gently pushed away their offer of help as he made his way toward his friend, the oak.

The great oak trembled in all its branches and reached out its light to embrace the man whom it loved. The old man stumbled but felt himself being uplifted by the enormous strength being given by the oak. He lay his staff against his old friend and raising his arms embraced the tree. His body was wracked by a huge sob. He could control his emotion no longer. He spoke:

"I have returned home my beloved friend. My work is now done in the world of men and I have come home as I promised I would." He sank down onto his knees. "In all my years amongst men you have never left me, but I have told of you to those who would understand, and as I promised when the time was ripe I would bring them to you, my dear friend."

The great oak was so overcome with joy that he could not reply, but a reply was not necessary for his light was so powerful that the men and women had to shield their eyes and when they looked again it was as if the man who had become their teacher had merged into the tree. It was as if physically they had become one. And from the light came that beautiful and glorious sound that had not been heard for so many, many years. As the sound grew every animal, bird and insect added their own sound; the sun shone more brightly and with a greater clarity as had never been seen before. It was as if time had slowed down and a state of bliss descended on the people.

For days the new community of people sat entranced before the great oak. The man with the dark eyes disappeared leaving the great oak radiating a light so transcendent that each man, tree, animal, insect and bird became one. None could tell who was who. Each tree was a man, each man was a tree, each a reflection of the other. Then it was that the great oak disappeared in a blaze of colour and in its place stood the man, tall and powerful and brilliant! A wonderful radiance of colour leapt around him that reached out so wide that the whole community of men, women, children and trees were as if on fire and their ecstasy was beyond words.

Then suddenly the trance was broken by a terrible groaning. A sound so awful that even the trees tasted fear for the first time for they had never heard a tree *die* before. Their beloved friend and teacher, the great oak, suddenly *split*!! A great crack appeared across its huge trunk and a cry so terrible rent the air that every man, woman and child covered their ears. The great oak was dying and even as it died spoke for the last time:

"My brothers, trees and humans, I and my brother, the man with the dark eyes, are one and it was always so. His task down amongst men is finished and my task amongst the trees is also finished. We all move over a sea of change. Nothing is permanent. Soon my body will lie hugging the ground where once I was placed as a child-seed by my beloved. Upon this spot you must build a temple from my body; for within that temple you will receive strength when strength you need, wisdom when wisdom is wanting, and love will be there for you always. Nothing is permanent save love. And my spirit and the spirit of the man will live on continuing to spread light and love in whatever form we are deemed to use it. Do not grieve for us, for we will be forever with you, forever *in* you. You are our inspiration for you will in turn inspire others."

The light from the oak diminished and with a great sigh that echoed throughout the forest this marvellous and beautiful tree started its journey to the ground. With a gigantic crash it came to rest. The crack that had appeared first was seen to be a clean cut as if an invisible axe had hewn it down with one mighty blow.

For nearly three weeks the men and women lived in the forest pitching their tents down amongst the spiral that had been planted by the man with the dark eyes, guided by the great oak, and they laboured night and day cutting the body of the oak into lengths and building a simple temple over the clean cut stump of the holy tree.

In time the stump became an altar and the

company of humans, the chosen ones of the man with the dark eyes, worshipped there and the elders amongst them took turns in its maintenance.

The chosen ones left the sacred forest to live further down the plain where the trees were more sparse, here they pitched their tents, here they sowed wheat brought with them from their days down in the world. Here they lived in harmony with the earth and with all things, tree and animal, and whenever strength and wisdom were needed then a visit to the temple on the summit was enough to set them on their course again.

The sacred forest of trees still looked to the summit where once their brother had stood, but even the temple made from the body of the oak gave forth a great light and was always a source of comfort to them.

In time the more enlightened humans went down into the world once again to show those who had survived the holocaust how to love and how to live in harmony, for the work of the man with the dark eyes must never end.

EVERY seven years after the death of the man and the great oak, that strange and beautiful sound could be heard ringing and toning through the forest filling each tree, animal and human with joy: a reminder of the wondrous being who had once walked amongst them; a reminder that all things come from love and all in time return to it

The great oak temple dedicated to the man with the dark eyes, stood on the summit of the plain for centuries, continuing to radiate light to the world; continuing to conquer darkness and spread love – for without love there is nothing.

NOTE: *1st edition: The Bosgo Press. (Illustrated)*
2nd edition: Thoth Publications. (Illustrated)
3rd edition: Honeytone Publications. (Illustrated)

PUSHING TIME

It was a long time ago, yet the experience still merges with the NOW. I am *still* talking about 'Oneness' with the One.

Only three times in my life, so far, have I ever got near to it. Yet I was merely scratching the surface of 'All That Is' during those incredible meditative states. I wanted *more*, but I could not achieve it, yet I still hear its echo, still savour the after-taste. I have been writing about it ever since (i.e. *The Stranger on the Threshold),* drawing on it for sustenance, inspiration, guidance and wisdom. I may have let that yapping dog 'ego' get in the way sometimes, but today's truth is tomorrow's half-truth, that much I have learned.

I was a master at 'pushing time': having to get things done by a certain period yet *knowing* that I had all the time in the world. If I could get through the day maybe tomorrow would be better, forgetting that *today* is *tomorrow's* past (eh?). Maybe the pain of *today* might disappear *tomorrow* without dealing with the pain NOW, today!

Somebody once said: "Do not follow where the path may lead, go, instead, where there is *no* path and leave a trail," difficult to leave a trail when you are living in the NOW. But that's not what living in the NOW is all about. You leave a trail IN THE NOW! Not yesterday, nor tomorrow, you live it NOW. Time may pass, yet you are *still* living in the NOW, yet *still* you leave a trail". *Time* is an illusion.

I'm not making any sense, am I? Look at it this way: one night I could fall asleep and dream of a complete lifetime: from a baby at my mother's breast, to a toddler, a complete childhood, teenager-hood, manhood, old age and finally death! Then I would wake up. Ten minutes had gone by! Ten minutes? Can you comprehend that? As a spiritual warrior you must have experienced that, or something like it.

They say that time is speeding up; even the young tell us that. What I am talking about is beyond mere time but living *in* a time zone simultaneously, at least until the frequency of the Earth speeds up enough for us to enter a Time-Free zone. But you don't have to wait until then! Okay, so appointments have to be kept. They *will* be.

Respect time. It *will* be respected! But don't knock yourself out, don't become a slave to it.

I remember a time when it all came together (I'm still knocking off the rough edges, mind you). I was travelling along in my car when it broke down. I was frantic! I had to give a lecture somewhere. Fortunately I broke-down beside a motorway telephone. I phoned the AA and was informed that I would have to wait at least half an hour!

Instead of worrying (as I am apt to do: a real energy sapper) a kind of peace settled upon me: I *knew* there was NOTHING I could do about the situation. It was a bright and beautiful day so I sat back and ENJOYED it. I listened to the radio, played some tapes and read the newspaper (not all at the same time) and just enjoyed myself.

When the AA-man arrived I found that he was as laid-back as I was. We chatted about his work at the *Rotary Club*, and suchlike, in all he was a great bloke. He called a garage on his mobile to order a breakdown lorry. When it arrived I climbed into the seat beside the driver and, having secured my vehicle, we were off to the garage. I was enjoying the ADVENTURE of it, relaxing *into* it.

Having just chatted to the AA-man and then had a conversation with the driver of the pickup truck, I then shared a cup-of-tea with the owner of the garage and the AA-man. I was REALLY enjoying myself. The AA-man was duty bound to take me to my door and so I arrived home safe and...happy!

Now if I had been frantic and uptight the story would have been *very* different. I had already phoned ahead to tell the organizers what had happened and that I would not be appearing: the people that had hired me for the lecture had found a stand-in and they hired me for another occasion.

I swore that from that time on, providing I *really could* do nothing about it, I was gonna go with the flow, fast or slow.

Time is not the enemy, WE are (t'was ever thus). I try to deal with my problems in the NOW. Sometimes I slip back into the old routine though, who doesn't? We all live in a three-dimensional Time Zone, but we don't *have* to abide by its seemingly strict rulings, do we?

Time is as addictive as any drug and it takes *Time* to wean us off, *Time* that features in the NOW. So make that decision...in the NOW!

NOTE: *first Published by NEW VISION.*

STONE CIRCLES IN SUDBURY

It has long been my belief, as many of you know, that some crop circles are formed on the very sites that the ancients built their stone complexes, harnessing and amplifying the natural *earth energy* that exists (and has been proven to exist, though we are still chipping way at the knowledge of what this natural earth energy can *really* do) at these sites and indeed many crop circles show this *very same* tendency of natural earth energy and, in some cases, healing.

In the book *JOEB – SERVANT OF GAIA*, I wrote in the *Introduction:* "On August 13th 1992, a group of twelve people sat in meditation. The idea was to give an invocation to the Earth Goddess (Gaia) in the hope that she might help us to understand the crop circle phenomenon. During our meditation I was overshadowed by a spiritual entity, who we later learned was called Joeb (actually he was called Djung, but that's another story). August 13th was a *very* wet and windy night and there was a full moon. Joeb spoke of vast changes that the planet would undergo, not only physically (10 years on we are *still* experiencing those changes), but through a gradual shift of consciousness to a higher frequency.

He spoke with compassion, understanding and love: *you called on my Lady, the Earth Goddess, whom I love and adore. I am her servant. You called Her and got me!"*

In the book *QUEST FOR CONTACT* (written by Andy Thomas and myself) Andy wrote: "At 8.00pm, with the storm hammering the window outside, the candles were put out and the group sat in silence and semi-darkness, turning the Sompting symbol over in their minds (the Sompting *crop circle* symbol found in a field of corn by St Mary's church. We had also gathered corn from the same site, which was strewn about the table). In thought, the crop patterns are freed from their two-dimensional cage and they can be twisted and turned in three-dimensional beauty. Many believe what we are seeing in our fields are simply flat representations of multi-dimensional energies and that we need to explore the designs in this way to unlock their secrets further.

Suddenly Paul's breathing increased rapidly and his posture changed. In the gloom, I could just see that his facial muscles were being unnaturally stretched as if they were taking on a new persona. Those who had never witnessed the like of what was about to occur looked up, startled. A voice suddenly cut through the groan of the wind outside, dry and ancient, quiet but commanding. Although I had known of Paul's 'gifts', I hadn't realised until then just what 'getting information' entailed. Now I knew; this

was what would have once been called a séance. The voice, speaking through Paul's vocal chords, delivered a disturbing message: (edited version)
The circles are just the beginning, planted by Man to make him think...or to make him scoff. The weather...strange. There will be much more. Man will be forced to know of what is to pass. Do not listen to those who scoff because within you, you know. This is very important. Nature is so powerful, so awe-inspiring. Man has made her angry; she is in pain. She is crying for help and you CAN help. You have work to do. I have seen the spirit of the earth in all Her beauty, brilliant and wonderful. I am privileged to bask in this. Look within yourselves, you will find Her there. There will be damage along this coastline; a little bit here; a little bit there. But you must not despair.

With these last words, Paul's breathing quietened again and all was still. His face was once again his own. Nobody said a word, stunned. "

(You must be wondering why I am quoting from these books. Don't worry, all will be revealed.)

Still quoting from *JOEB – SERVANT OF GAIA* I wrote: "On the 28th September 1993, on a grey, rainy day, David Russell (the dowser and archaeologist), Andy Thomas, Quenton Cole (my nephew) and I started on a journey to Sudbury in Suffolk, in search of the site of a stone henge that Joeb had told us about. Joeb wished to prove to us his existence as an ordinary underling priest, during the end of the first century and the beginning of the second century AD.

He had told us that the site was near water. The henge, he told us, consisted of two circles with a horseshoe shape in the middle. Although the henge itself would no longer be there, the energy points of where they once had stood would remain, and could be easily dowsed.

We knew the site was indeed near water, for when we map-dowsed the area and found the site it was close to the *River Stour*, which runs almost the entire length of Sudbury, near the *Downs Walk*. It was also only a couple of miles from *Borley*, once known as the most haunted place in England. Joeb told us that Borley Rectory, which was burned down in 1928, was on the site of an ancient temple that was once used as a Gateway between the worlds but was misused and became corrupt.

On the way to Sudbury we stopped for lunch where David and I decided to map-dowse for the *very* village where Joeb lived. We actually found it! We also found the site of the graveyard. We reasoned that we might just as well check it all out while we were at it!

We arrived at the site of Borley Hall. The *Downs Walk* meanders its way past the bottom of Borley Hall's driveway, then across country. I parked the car whilst the others gathered their dowsing tools and maps ready for the walk. I expected a long wait in the car. (I'm a polio person, and for me walking any distance is a no-no!) Suddenly Quenton came bounding back along the path. "You can drive right there," he said, sliding into the passenger seat, and we were off! As we drove along Andy and David loomed into view. David had already picked up the direction, and within only a few minutes the dowsing rods were pointing at a ploughed field; a field where, incidentally, I could park facing the area where we believed Joeb's stones once stood.

Quenton got there first following the far perimeter of the field. I could see him clearly, waiting for David and Andy to catch up. Little did I, or Quenton, know that he was standing almost exactly in the middle of where Joeb's stones once stood!

I *tuned in* and felt a wave of excitement. Joeb told me that *this was the place!*

After half an hour they returned to the car. "The outer circle is 30m wide," said David, wiping the mud from his boots. "The inner circle is about 10m, but we couldn't get near the centre because there's a ditch." (Joeb had told us the outer circle had energy running anticlockwise, the inner circle ran clockwise, but in the centre the stones were shaped like a horseshoe. This was known as the *Seat of Power*.) Later we map-dowsed the site and found the outer circle had nine stones, the inner eight stones, and the *Seat of Power* had five stones, exactly as Joeb had told us in a previous meeting. (See illustration.)

We then decided to find the site of Joeb's village (which was known as *Orik*). We found the site only a few miles away. Without permission from the farmer, we decided not to get too close to the site of the village, but the site of the graveyard (a ploughed field) was very typical of a Celtic graveyard, on a slope near water. The field curved down to the *River Stour* below.

We had all brought posies of flowers as a gift to the guardian of the stone circle, and also to the Earth Goddess herself. We had only one posy left. We intended to dowse for Joeb's grave and place the flowers on top of it as a gesture of respect! In the car Joeb spoke. "I appreciate the gesture, my friends, but it was a long time ago. The bones of that body are no longer there. You have done well today. Now you have a little proof of my existence, and I thank you all for your work."

In his interview with Joeb on 21/9/93, Michael Green stated in his *notes:*

"No Stonehenge-like monuments have ever been recorded this far east in England, and if they ever existed they must have been rarer than those recorded in the north and west. However, it is possible that the glacial erratics from the Boulder Clay could have been used for constructional purposes. The monument, as described by Joeb, is unusually complex (even of its type) with its double ring and central 'cove', as archaeologists term this particular feature. The nearest surviving examples are to be found in the Derbyshire group, and in particular at Arbor Low which has a 'cove' and continued as a focus of local worship into the Bronze Age."

NOW READ ON

A reader (Christine Rudderham) sent to Andy Thomas and I the following cutting from the *EAST ANGLIAN DAILY TIMES*. The central feature of the story tells us that eleven sarsens, boulders made from sandstone, have been seen in the grounds of St Barnabas Church, Alphamstone, near SUDBURY in Suffolk! (Christian churches were usually built on or over the site of pagan religion, thereby superimposing *their* beliefs over that of the pagans!) Experts now think that they have discovered a miniature Stonehenge. They went on to say: *sarsens are not rare but geologists believe the collection at Alphamstone is the largest outside Wiltshire, home to the famous Stonehenge and several other renowned formations.* The article concluded that: *the rocks were formed in Britain's hot climate of more than twenty million years ago, and were then swept through the STOUR VALLEY during the Ice Age.* Group chairman, Gerald Lucy, of the Heritage group, ESSEX Rigs, said: *"Although several sarsen rocks can be seen scattered around, a formation like this is UNIQUE IN THE REGION. It is without doubt the largest collection recorded outside Wiltshire."*

Although this might not be *conclusive* proof (dowsing is a dodgy art, no matter how good you are) of the fact that Joeb existed in another life as a kind of *Priest of the Stones*, at least the *material* existed whereby his people, or people like him, could build these marvellous stone complexes.

I conclude with what I started with: the notion that certain patterns already existing in the ground are activating and bringing down the crops to produce these marvellous *Patterns of Power*. For that is what they are and *nobody* can tell me otherwise! And why NOW? *You* tell *me*, for I think in your heart of hearts that you *know* the answer to that question.

The book: STEPPING TO THE DRUMMER The Extraordinary Tales of a Psychic Man with a Foreword by *Uri Geller,* contains the original conversation, word for word, with Michael Green and Joeb.

NOTE: *First published on the website:* **SWIRLED NEWS**

THE STRANGER ON THE THRESHOLD

The wood seemed to embrace the man, or he *it*. Whatever was happening he *wanted* it, he wanted it with all his heart, soul and being. It was consuming him and he *wanted* to be consumed, eaten up, to become *One With The All*, he thirsted for it, hungered for it, he wanted it to take him lock, stock and barrel, he wanted it to make him *clean*, to clear him out of all he possessed, to make him spiritually *light* where now he was so *heavy*. The man wanted this experience so badly that it hurt. The pain was unbearable.

Surely this obsession, for that's what it was, was a DESIRE and he had been taught to curb *desire*. The man became confused, bewildered. There was this voice telling him that it was *wrong*. How could it be wrong?

Then another voice: BALANCE. He had also been taught that *balance in all things* was the Path to Freedom.

The man's head was fit to explode. Tears coursed down his cheeks, hot tears, bitter tears, tears of confusion and frustration. His face crumpled with the agony of what to do. *Balance* meant the 'middle way' and the 'middle way' meant that he was to *observe* without getting emotionally involved: "Stand away from that that you desire without attachment!" What did *that* mean? He couldn't do it, he *thought* that he could, the written word said that he could, but to put it into practice?

It clawed at him still, the feeling that he wanted to join, to become the woods themselves, could that be so bad? He had wanted to attain Oneness all his life and here it was loud and clear, the beckoning hand that he had sought all these years. But a voice inside of him cried: *Restraint! You are not ready. Tread the middle way. Observe the beauty, just OBSERVE Oneness!*

He couldn't, the feeling was too strong, too urgent. He screamed with the pain and frustration of all that was happening to him. Yet all the while was aware of a Being, just out of view, that was watching him, it didn't attempt to come to his rescue, didn't try to help him, just remained calm and observing. He was only just aware of the Being, but he remembered the Being in the recesses of his memory, but then it closed up, the memory gone.

The wave of Light piled over the man, swamped him, carrying him along with it. It seemed to carry him forever, through mountains and rains and forests; huge winds buffeted him, punched him and yet he was in ecstasy. The water came up to meet him, greet him, and when it had drenched him threw him down a gully, and a river then took him over rocks. Fear did not touch him...for now.

The river took him out to sea and he knew what it was to swim with the fishes. He saw all manner of mammal, knew intimately every shark and whale, each tiny plankton, jellyfish swam in and out of his *heart* so that he loved them beyond all things, loved ALL the creatures of the sea FOR THEY *ALL* SWAM TO HIS HEART!

Then the currents took him and washed him up on the shore. He walked through jungles and swung from tree to tree with monkeys and apes, wriggled with snakes, roared with lions, laughed with the hyena FOR THEY *ALL* CAME TO HIS HEART!

Then a wind took him and he was flying with all variety of bird: vulture, sparrow, eagle, seagull, he soared with them all FOR THEY *ALL* CAME TO HIS HEART!

And finally he *became the woods*, and he found that trees gave him an experience that was, to him, the greatest experience of them all: for all trees feel *all* what he had felt and they too take *all to their heart:* trees take water up to their *centre* and all that water contains; animals take shelter beneath their canopies and rub themselves against their trunks when they have the need to scratch; big cats mark their territory; monkeys swing from their branches; birds perch and make their nests; the wind blows through their structures, making a sound that only trees can make; the rain lashes them; hail bombards them and when winter comes, snow transforms them into white, gentle-like people, the snow has a habit of making all trees seem alike.

But then came the *fear*, but not fear like any he had known, this was an intangible fear, an indescribable wall of fear, a *being* of sheer terror that began to consume him, leak into him, eat away at him from the inside! It began with small tremors that surprised him, after all, the sense of ecstasy was only just beginning to subside, to leave him. What *was* this?

The fear increased in its intensity. He felt like he was going insane. He was *afraid* of being *afraid*, afraid of the fear! How could this be? Then it left him almost as suddenly as it had begun. Had he dreamt it, ALL of it?

The sun was setting in the wood; long shadows cast their spell amidst golden pools of light where the rain had gathered. The smell of evening has an odour all its own: bluebells oozing the last of their perfume and the late daffodils with their earthy, sweet, breath mingled with early, wild dog rose. The wood floor was soft and springy underfoot with leaf mould that had been scattered from a thousand trees, which gave off a decaying, yet rich and beautiful smell that was characteristic of nowhere else but a wood or forest.

Although the man had indeed experienced Oneness, felt that ecstatic Love and Compassion for All things he also *knew* that he had only just brushed the face of the Infinite, looked oh so briefly into the eyes of the One. And yes he *did* feel lighter, more complete...and yet.

Doubt clouded his mind again; fear flickered and played with him. He tried to remember what he had heard some wise man say, some sage. What was it? He tried to recall but it wouldn't come. The fear came now thick and strong: the trees seemed to reach out for him, claw him in an evil embrace; he saw faces in their bark, hideous faces that opened their mouths as if to consume him. Where at one time he had *wanted* to be consumed, this time they made as if to tear his flesh, eat him alive, even the ground seem to grip him, opening up as his feet sank into the soft leaf mould and as he sank down the stench of evil and foulness overcame him, he couldn't breathe, he was suffocating he was drowning in the ground!

When he came to he was lying outstretched on the floor of the wood, his hands dug into the soft soil. At first he thought that he had dreamt it, *all* of it: the agony AND the ecstasy. It was then that he remembered what the sage had said: *"You must let go of all that you have created in this life and before this life, you must let go of the creature you have encountered or it will rise up and attack you. This creature is called THE STRANGER ON THE THRESHOLD. You will recognise this stranger through intense fear, and you will also know that YOU CREATED IT through your thoughts and deeds, and through indulging the EGO. Yes, even the path to Enlightenment is filled with ego!"*

Night came, and the creatures of the night came out: rats, voles, mice, bats. The fear had abated and he accepted these small creatures as a part of the wood, even the trees in their shadowy garb he accepted without the insane fear that had gripped him. He made his way through moonlit mounds of grass, toward the brook. He was just crossing the water, over the old small wooden bridge that spanned the stream, when he noticed a figure. The figure didn't alarm him, didn't cause him to have a spasm of fear because he *knew* him, or at least knew *of* him. It was the figure that he had seen out of the corner of his eye during the wrestle with his mind, the figure that he had seen before he experienced Oneness, the figure that had remained completely *still*, the figure that had just *observed* his ecstasy AND, he now knew, his pain. Now the figure could be seen clearly in the light of the moon.

But the figure kept *changing* from that of a man with a beard and a turban with flowing robes to a woman with long, fair hair. The man not only saw them change but *felt* them change, from a poet to a musician, from a fisherman to a prostitute, from a traveller to a sailor to a seamstress with a hoard of tiny children to a man of science and throughout all of these lives he sought to know how to love, the meaning of love in all its colours and flavours, all its twists and turns, until he had distilled it into a pure unconditional substance beyond thought and beyond reason, beyond anything that he could have imagined. The figure reached out to the man, this figure of pure love, reached out with its arms. And the figure glowed with a light that wasn't of this world but all the worlds that ever were and ever would be.

The man rubbed his eyes. Surely this being was an angel brought down from the heavens. Suddenly, and without warning, he was dealt a mighty blow of fear that shook him to the very foundation of his being. The fear magnified and took hold of him, and he screamed with terror and agony and clutched his abdomen, crashing to his knees on the little wooden bridge. In that moment he thought of taking his own life.

He was dying, he couldn't take it anymore it was too painful. Throughout all his pain the words of the old sage came back to him: *"You will recognise this stranger through intense fear, and you will also know that YOU CREATED IT through your thoughts and deeds.* The man also remembered words that he had forgotten: *"Face your fear head on, resistance is pain!!* The words of the old sage echoed round and round: *"Resistance is pain...resistance is pain..."*

He had nothing left to give. The man was dying. If resistance *was* pain then he had nothing to lose. With a mighty act of will and courage he let the fear take over his body, he gave in to this creature that he had created, gave in to its seeming evil, let it take him, kill him, if that's what it took.

But the moment that he let go of it, *it* let go of *him*. He felt peace enter his body, a calmness and strength that he had never known before. But he also knew that he hadn't got rid of it *entirely*. No, that would take time, but he knew that he could do it, realised that he could beat it, dismantle it brick by brick, as he had built it up in the first place. The creature that he had created was born of *all* the lives that he had lived over thousands of years.

He looked up, the figure was still there, still radiant, still full of love and compassion and understanding. Realisation dawned. He had thought that he recognised the figure from the start, from the beginning of his journeyings but he couldn't quite make out who he was. He thought he recognised the women too. Yes, oh yes, they were all part of *him*; *all* the lives were part of HIM! He *was* the figure. And he realised this also: that he could *not* die, *need* not die, that all of this life now stretched before him. Time enough, he thought, to iron out the defects, to make good his relationships, time enough to *serve*, but above all time enough: *to love*, the quality that he had sought for so many, many lives.

The figure waited quietly and patiently, arms still outstretched.
But it would have to wait for just a little longer,
The man had things to do
That just couldn't wait.

LOVE IS ALL THERE IS

The above title is all you really need to know – or is it? The journey and devotion to *love* is a hard road, a long and hard road. But the rewards are also long and hard, for they go deep, much deeper than you know, in fact they become a part of you, part of your very nature. Don't try and look beyond your nose but look *within*. Yes, I know all that New Age stuff about looking within, you can become sick and tired of hearing it, BUT IT'S A TRUTH, believe me.

Look at it this way: the Truth, say, is locked up inside a stone. The way to Truth is to crack the stone open, but what do you find? More stone. The thing is to change your very nature, through and through, every last vestige of you, but you have eternity to do it in, time being an illusion and time IS an illusion.

The way is sometimes painful, sometimes more painful than you can bear. You then fragment, leaving splinters of that pain, hiding those fragments of pain until you can stand it no longer. This type of pain can, and does, fester if held within your self. But even pain can be transformed into joy. Your wounds can be bound with happiness. Like that stone when cut, splinters into fragments. Even though your *intent* is correct and true.

So how can it benefit you by looking within? Simple, you have to look in the right direction and the right direction is your *heart*. You have to look after the *physical* heart or it gets clogged up and malfunctions: right food, right drink, correct exercises, all contribute to a healthy heart. So it is with the spiritual *heart:* right thought, right action, right spiritual exercises, and at the very centre Love and Compassion for *everything.* Easy? No, it's not easy. You try and love somebody that sneers at you, or makes fun of you, or beats you up and wages war on you. It's so much easier to look after the physical heart, after all, you just feed it the right nutrients, give it a little regular exercise. To love somebody who is your enemy is very, very hard. How do you do it? By not reacting, by not rising to their bait, even though anger is bursting in your breast to get out, or fear is making you cower. Do not react. Just take a few deep breaths and walk away, *sending out love to the person concerned as you go.* Not easy.

Coming to grips with Love is an *abstraction* until you can *really* understand it (Love). Then, after a seeming betrayal: a sudden death of somebody close, or worse, the brutal murder of a child, suddenly Love becomes an abstraction once again and you become frustrated and disillusioned and leave off the spiritual practises. But then you realise that Love runs as deep as pain, and they surface *together*. Love, like pain, never lets you go, except that Love *heals* the pain and absorbs it into itself. The death of a child is hard to understand and even karmic law (action and reaction) makes little sense until you realise that life is a continuous stream, ever running on into the universe until it becomes a river, and then a sea, filling the *whole* cosmos and beyond.

The stream of life never ends. All religions are caught up in this stream of life and all are watered down until there is nothing left but Love itself, because *Love Is All There Is*, Love is the sum total of it.

Love can be splinters of rock, or the petals of a flower, the air we breathe or the language we learn, the wings of a bird, or the fins of a fish swimming toward freedom.

When you no longer have a name you will have arrived! But don't think that it ends there. THERE IS NO END. All that comes after is a bonus, and that bonus is...that bonus is the great mystery of the Eternal itself, and I for one *thrive* on mysteries.

The journey is the *all*. The trick (or treat) of the journey is *never to arrive*.

KARMA.

"And Love Said: In the autumn of my years when things begin to stiffen and stifle, when I can eat only fruit and trifle and rifle through what might have been. The scene is not to look back and lack the means to put it right. For Love is forever youthful and truthful, never trite. For as the shadows of life grow long and you sing Love's song, though silent on your lips, and mouth the words: LOVE, it roars and it roars down the years until you cry for joy and say: this is what it is! This is what it is!" From the book: *"AND LOVE SAID...THE ORACLE."* Quote number 225.

Karma goes round and round like a merry-go-round and cries out "Had enough pain yet, had enough sorrow, because if you haven't learnt the lesson I'll be back tomorrow?" **Change**, why don't you, get off the merry-go-round. To be dizzy is to be confused. You *can* do it. What was it, in that film? You know the one, where the central character cries **Freedom!** *'Braveheart'* that's what it was called. You have to have a *brave heart.*

We are all afraid of *change*. Yet all we have to do is put a foot down and stop the merry-go-round. *Instant Karma.*

Tell me, have you *ever* had anything in your life that has turned out as bad as your *imagination* has created? There are exceptions of course. But can 99% of you put up their hands and say: "It never turned out quite as bad as I thought it would," have you? Imagination can be a terrible thing. It can also be a *wonderful* thing. After all, imagination and *inspiration* created all manner of things: from a simple garden to a poem, painting, song or a piece of sculpture. All, ALL are products of the imagination.

Fear also plays a part in the power of the imagination, a dreadful part, and it's a hard thing to stop in the merry-go-round of things. But that is where Love comes in. You have to work on your fear with Love. It's easy for me to say, isn't it? I remember a time during a meditation when I, for once in my life, touched *Oneness*. When all things seemed to merge into one golden whole and I was a *part* of that wholeness. I couldn't wait for my next meditation. But when it didn't happen, I thought that I was fooling myself, and my imagination was playing tricks on me. But no, a week later it happened again. I wasn't dreaming after all. And a week after that it happened again, and I *knew* that it was a reality, as real as this word processor, but even *more* so. I had touched the face of the Infinite for a nano-second *and I wanted more.*

But then I experienced the reverse side of the coin. Where bliss surrounded me there was fear, intense fear (see: *The Stranger on the Threshold*). Fear so real that for a moment I thought of taking my life...but only for a moment. In retrospect I knew that it was a breaking down of my old self, the self I had created, the part of me that I no longer needed: the *Ego Self*. Of course we all need a piece of ego in order to survive, but my ego had become out of control. I became *afraid of being afraid*.

Eventually I learned that *resistance* is pain. I had fought so hard against this fear that I became exhausted and weary. If it had to *'take me'* then so be it. I just didn't care anymore.

I called the Self that I had created **Charley**. I *named* it. And slowly but surely it left me. I wouldn't wish that experience on anybody, ANYBODY. But I have been drawing on that experience ever since, BOTH experiences. The dregs of fear haven't quite left me yet, but it keeps me on my toes.

I haven't yet brought the 'merry-go-round of *karma'* to a halt just yet, but I'm getting there, and so can YOU. Remember that 'pay back time' is NOW if you're not careful. Be careful *not* to put yourself in that position, in the 'pay back' position unless it's of the positive, loving kind. Then the Kingdom of Heaven will pay you a visit, you can bet your sweet arse on it!

JOURNEY FROM ALPHA TO OMEGA... AND BACK

It is said that when a *great soul* passes into so-called death that they become absorbed into *All That Is*. Souls such as the Buddha, Ghandi, Jesus but also aspiring souls, such as Treya Wilber, whose story is so beautifully (and movingly) told in Ken Wilber's book "Grace and Grit".

I wrote a poem years ago a line of which read: *"when I no longer have a name then I too would merge with the Eternal"*. This is what I believe but in truth when I have come close to God, to *Oneness*, and merely touched the Eternals face I have suffered horribly for my pains: after the *ecstasy* the *agony*. Yet I *still* hunger for that moment of ecstasy. I say *hunger*, it's a gentle hunger now, more a sense of: *when it happens it happens*. Yes, let me get a little bit more spiritual awareness under my soul's belt, then we'll see.

Now my questions are these: when we merge with *All That Is* and finally let go of the world and all that's in it do we really lose our identity? Can we still be found in the stillness on a lake; the wind; the rain; the trees and all that grows; the soul of a planet etc? Or can we re-emerge as a single entity again, coming and going as we please in service? And what of the great *White Brotherhood,* are these *aspects* of the *real* masters, each one representing a part of the whole? Or are we missing the point somehow?

I suspect that they ARE yet still keeping a toe dipped in the sea of *All That Is.* They come again to help Man/Womankind, help in their spiritual struggles, help to become what they are themselves: *THE ETERNAL PRESENCE,* and help us not to trip over, but if we do, help us to our feet again and lead the way out of this spiritual maze, having trod the *agony* and the *joy* themselves, having come to that searing conclusion that it was all worth while.

Having said that, it's still a wonderful journey that we're on, because a journey, or adventure, is what it is: an incredible yet painful *adventure* back to our SELVES, back to the God that spawned us in the first place!

We all stand up and fall over again and it's these wonderful beings from whom we seek wisdom, these wonderful beings that will gently, though not *always* gentle, haul us to our feet and point us in the right direction, beings that are always there for us.

It doesn't matter a hoot what religion you are, it doesn't matter if you adjure to no religion at *all* as long as you *serve* each other with *love, compassion and kindness* these are all you need! Whether you serve the Nature God, *Pan*, or the Sun God, *Ra*, they are all *aspects* of the One.

But how do we know what path to take? How do we know what teacher to follow? In my experience, if you truly *want* it, they make an appearance at the *right* time and in the *right* place. A poem could point the way, but it doesn't mean that THAT poet is your teacher. A phrase or comment in a newspaper or magazine will set your spirit on fire, but that doesn't mean you should take notice of the whole article. Something that someone says, or something that someone does, the sound of a piece of music, a particular smell that evokes a memory of something or someone that you've forgotten. It really doesn't matter. They are *all* signposts. And then your teacher, as if by magic, will appear.

Teachers come in many guises: the man or woman next door; a particular author; a composer; a person who, up to that particular time, you had taken *no* notice of because you deemed him or her *not worth listening* to, but now you realise that they have something to say that is of great value to you simply by something that they said and *how* they said it. That's important: *how* they said it. Or a face in a crowd that fills you to the very brim with compassion and love...but you don't know why; by listening *for the very first time* to an aunt or uncle, or your own *mother,* yes, your own mother or father, those people that are, seemingly, *so un-cool.* It can take a long time to listen to your folks, to wake up to the fact that even *they* are capable of wisdom and insight!

But in choosing *the* Teacher, well, that's up to you. When you've followed all the little resonating signposts (and they will *still* continue to wave at you) they will all merge into a kind of *whole,* but if you choose to continue *listening* to God, or whatever you deem to call this great universal power, through the medium of the poets, musicians, aunts and uncles, etc. you will have of course already have *cracked* it. For you have ALREADY chosen, you are *recognising* TRUTH and truth *is* the Eternal One: the God of Love and Compassion!

NOTE: *First published on NEW VISION.*

INFINITE HUMOUR
(for Spike Milligan)

On February 27th 2002 one of my heroes's died, Sir Spike Milligan: humorist, satirist, humanitarian and vegetarian; he went from this place of war, anger and mistrust.

He wasn't a perfect man by any means but as a clown supreme he was a genius in the art of *laughter*, even though he suffered horribly with manic depression brought on by severe shellshock during the 2nd World War where he served as a gunner. Only in later years did he discover the antidepressant Lithium. He said, characteristically: "When I die I want carved on my headstone: "*I told you I was ill!*"

This piece is not exactly about Spike but rather about the Infinites' *relationship* with humour. Michael Bentine, author of *"The Long Banana Skin"* *"A Door Marked Summer"*, a book of very high spiritual value (in my opinion) and *"The Doors Of The Mind"* was a close friend of Spike Milligan (Michael was a fellow founder of 'The Goon Show' of which Spike was the writer and creator) and more than implied that *"laughter, not bread, was the staff of life!"* In fact it has been proved that laughter can *HEAL*: when a patient in hospital (or anywhere, come to that) is exposed to laughter, whether it be on television or radio or whatever, they heal more quickly. Also when spirit healers are allowed into hospitals after an operation -with the patients permission, of course- the results are similar.

When I start a poetry reading I always begin with what I call the *icebreakers*, poems that are guaranteed to make folk howl with laughter (well, not always but 95% of the time) thus paving the way for more serious, philosophical poems. I've been doing it for 30 years or more, so I should know. I usually start with one of *two* poems. For the sake of space within this piece I shall reshape this poem into standard prose, the title of this poem is: *When I Was An Arcade Cashier*. "I was surrounded by pyramids of pennies; entombed in a glass booth like a Houdini death-trap, bashing out change to the arcade punters. A little girl approached. She looked up at me, eyes wide with wonder. "What does it do?", she said. It dawned on me: she thought I was a machine! Using my best Dalek dialect I replied: "Put your penny through the hole in the glass." Without hesitation she plunged her tiny hand into her tiny, plastic purse and produced a penny. She pushed it through the hole. Doing impressions of a robot I mechanically picked up the penny. I then did the best 'Laughing Policeman' send-up that I'd ever done: I roared with laughter, my face like a ripe plum, I swayed this way and that jerking like an idiot. I reasoned that a full minute was enough and came to an abrupt end. I was shattered! The little girl was dazed with dizzy amazement, her eyes as wide as her mouth. She paused. Then plunging her hand Into her tiny plastic purse she produced yet *another* penny! Three pennies was all she had and three pennies was all I needed...for my first professional engagement!"

"Roy Castle, tap dancer, musician, humorist and Christian told this story: He was working at a club, or some other venue, and he had to catch a late train home. He'd just sat down when a man, obviously the worse for drink after some sort of celebration and carrying a briefcase plus an umbrella, entered the carriage. He was dishevelled and he had drink stains down the front of his crumpled, though well cut, (and he was *well* cut) suit. He put the umbrella and briefcase in the overhead baggage hold, sat down and promptly fell asleep. He'd been asleep for about 15 minutes when the train came to a sudden halt for no known reason (as they do). With that he woke up, took his umbrella and briefcase out of the 'overhead' opened the door and stepped out! Well, being British, nobody said anything. Then a hand appeared with an umbrella in it, and then another hand appeared and he hauled himself *and* the briefcase back into the carriage. He slurred: "You must think I'm an awful fool," and promptly opened the OTHER door and stepped out!" (Pause for laughter?)

"I once bought an old Standard.8. car. It was a rust-bucket but the engine was sound and I set to work rubbing it down and HAND PAINTING it! It was a sight to behold: all shiny and, in its way, NEW looking. I was very proud of that car which I had laboured over. Anyway, my girlfriend and I decided to go to the pictures. We'd just pulled up outside the cinema when a policeman approached. "Is this *your* car, sir?" he said. "Well, yes officer," I said proudly. "Are you parking it 'ere, sir?" the policeman continued, "well, yes officer." "Oh, that's alright, sir, for a moment I thought you were dumping it!" The thing was: HE WAS SERIOUS!"

All three stories are perfectly true. Can't you see the absurdity of it all? Life is a game and we are merely the players taking on different roles in order to learn *and* to enjoy ourselves. The spiritual life is the *same*. Sometimes we tend to take it all too seriously. Life is an abstract *joy* as well as a *game*. It all depends on the way you *play* the game. Spike Milligan suffered too for his humour, and after a serious breakdown he decided that the *Elfin Oak* in Kensington Gardens needed restoration and an overhaul. All those little pixies and gnomes needed repainting and a bit of tree surgery. So as therapy after this severe trauma he set to work. After a while he was recognised, so he put up screens. "He's just been let out of a loony bin, he's raving mad," he heard someone say. This depressed Spike even more but he was determined to finish the task he had set himself...because it was for CHILDREN, and he *loved* children. Even his own children he used to leave tiny notes under various stones in his garden and tell them it was *from the fairies*, he used to write them at night on tiny bits of paper in minuscule writing and put them in equally tiny envelopes. When all his children were asleep, he'd creep into the garden and deposit them. He *loved* children and he *loved* making people laugh, even though at times it was an awful strain. I remember him telling a story about his little girl, Laura, who was playing in the back garden with some other kids. Spike had decided to use their garden toilet. Suddenly there was a knock at the toilet door, "who is it?" said Spike, "It's somebody else," came the reply. Spike convulsed with laughter at the memory: "only children could say that," he said. Spike wrote professionally for children, too. Julian Young a journalist friend of mine said: "I had one of his books called *"A BIT OF A BOOK OR A BOOK OF BITS"*. The book actually *did* fall into bits as I thumbed it so often. The poems were so *unlike* anything that I had read at school."

I shall miss him terribly, but although he was not a spiritual man in the conventional sense, in a way *he was*. He left us a legacy of laughter that is as precious as any holy text and now he's going to make even the angels laugh...don't tell him I told you, though.

The Infinite gave to us this unique ability to laugh at ourselves. Laughter is the balm of the Gods; if laughter is not present I, for one, don't want anything to do with it.

Doctor Love said: *"Open your mouth and say OMMMM."*
(Well, it makes *me* laugh, anyway.)

(*Just in case you don't understand the joke- I feel sure that you do- OMMMM is a spiritual mantra.*)

IDLE HANDS

What shall I do now? I've made the treacle pudding for Sunday lunch (popped it in the microwave and set it for 4 minutes. All I have to do now is *switch on*. When it *dings* it's *done!*). I've dallied with the idea of painting my 4-foot model *powerboat* (5cc) with another coat of black *sealer*. No, I'll do that after lunch...if I can *move!* Bura lunches can be, and often are, belly-bashers, and if I'm not careful I'll fall asleep. I've done what washing-up there is (after the making of the treacle pud) and now I have a couple of hours to *WRITE*. But what shall I write about? I've finished writing *'THE LOVE ORACLE'* (a kind of dowsers *I Ching*. You dowse for an answer to a given question and it provides you with the answer) and I've sent it off to a publisher. I've finished **'HERNE BAY: The Little Restaurant on the Prom'** and sent it off to Beth my editor to check before it too goes to a publisher. Whether they'll except *either* of them or not is another matter!

So what *shall* I write about? I know, I'll write about *writing*. That's it, I'll write about what has consumed me for most of my life. BORING, you say. Hmm. Well for the *writers* among you it probably aint.
I've written most of my life, mostly poetry. It was 12 years before I found my first London

publisher, until then I'd published myself. I was, no AM, a performing poet. The poetry bug seems to me to be the best way that I could, or can, express myself. I've written seven collections in all. Then, for some reason, known only to the Infinite, I stopped writing for *ten* years. Then I moved to Sussex.

I got caught up in the crop circle phenomena. I did a poetry reading for the 'croppies' and got such a warm response that I started writing poetry again.

Meanwhile, I was *also* contributing articles to *SC. Magazine* (a crop circle bi-monthly), *The Quarterly* and *The Science of Thought Review*, little spiritual and philosophical magazines.

Then Andy Thomas invited me to co-write with him *QUEST FOR CONTACT*, about our experiences with the crop circles and how we, by creative imagination and sound, managed to create a pattern in the corn, and my roll as a psychic in all of this.

My psychic abilities and adventures, which are *still* continuing, are all related in my book *STEPPING TO THE DRUMMER*, with a foreword by *Uri Geller*.

I'm very lucky in that occasionally I get published. I learned my craft the hard way. I could paper a room with all my reject slips. But I refused to let go. I *had* something to say. I *still* have something to say.

My life has been marred by polio, and then 45 years later a tumour the size of an orange was plucked from my brain. I'm lucky that it was benign. But as a result I'm now epileptic. But my 'fits' are held in check by liquid insulation tape. I.E. drugs. But I can *still* write. Those shapes on clean white paper are a continual joy to me, a luxury. Even scribbled words and phrases written on old recites when a poem is forming, screaming for birth, shouting at me to take notice of it, are a wonder of the creation process.

Yet who is writing? Who is in charge? Sometimes (as most writers experience) it is the *process* that is writing *me*. Which is not to say that I have not any *personal* talent. I like to think that I have...and yet.

But are we not all connected to a central computer, *the Infinite*? And have we not all a certain talent of some sort? Mine just happens to be *writing*.

I happen to believe that we are ALL interconnected by our chakric systems and when the mass of us happen to build up or recognise a certain *truth* within our selves then we *all* recognise it at once. Of course not *everyone* recognises that *truth*. *Time* is *change*, and we don't all change at once. But once that *truth* is logged-in to the chakric system it's only a matter of course before it kicks in, and only if it is OF THE LIGHT! And if it isn't 'of the Light' then we have a choice. We either reject it or except it, it's as simple and *devastating*, as that!

Dr Rupert Sheldrake in his theory of *Morphic Resonance,* found that a group of monkeys decided to wash the sand and dirt off of their fruit in the sea before eating it. Meanwhile, hundreds of miles away, *another* group of monkeys decided to *do the very same thing*! If the monkeys decided that it was a BAD thing then they would have discontinued the practice. Coincidence? I think not. Coincidence is merely *cause* and *effect.* As I have already said: *Time* equates as *Change,* no matter how *long* it takes; the pebble thrown in the pond ripples out (*cause*), and when it hits the edge of the pond (the *effect*) it cannot help but cause a change, no matter how small.

(Mother's calling us for Sunday lunch: pushes button on microwave!)

We had toad-in-the-hole (veggie style) *with thick, brown gravy, roast potatoes, carrots and spring greens...and of course, treacle pudding* for dessert!

FREEDOM

"To seek freedom is the only driving force I know. Freedom to fly off into that infinity out there. Freedom to dissolve; to lift off; to be like the flame of a candle which, in spite being up against the light of a billion stars, remains intact, because it never pretended to be more than what it was: a mere candle." Don Juan Matus.

In his series of books about Don Juan Matus, a Mexican Yaqui Indian sorcerer, Carlos Castaneda tells of his terror and of his joy. Sometimes he hated Don Juan but most times he *loved* him. He hated him because Don Juan put him through a series of tests that would drive the average man insane. Carlos believed he *was* an average man. But Don Juan Matus saw in this average man something else. And taught him all manner of things to make him realise that *freedom* was the ALL. And always, *always* he gets a little nearer to that *freedom*.

To become a *spiritual warrior,* as Don Juan described it, the one thing that is *all*-important is to stop the *inner dialogue,* the rubbish that is the chattering monkeys in your head, always talking, talking, and talking. Until you can find that *still place within* and just *be* you can't do anything, you can't get anywhere. I don't mean completely. That would be asking too much! But until you can *let go of your ego* and put aside the monster that ego can create, *freedom* will always evade you.

You have to finally kill the monster that your senses (ego) have created (***see THE STRANGER ON THE THRESHOLD***) You can do this, for instance, when you feel that your world is collapsing about you, but collapsing in-as-much as the 'old' welcoming the 'new'. You will find that you no longer have to *prove* this or that either physically, emotionally, or spiritually.

But this is not without much pain. But at the end of it you will be *free!* You may feel that the Infinite has deserted you (just as Jesus on the cross thought that the Infinite had deserted *him*), that you are alone. Nothing is further from the truth. Once you have recognised the Infinite for what it is: *ALL LOVE*, and once you have excepted that fact as a reality, that Love is *within* you and will *never let you go*, then, and only then, will you be *free.*

Enjoy the good times as well as you can tolerate the bad times. They are all lessons in the scheme of things. But you already *know* that, otherwise you wouldn't be reading this book. Let's call it a little reminder.

Freedom can mean many things. *Freedom* from a nasty marriage ending in divorce; *freedom*

from jail; *freedom* from mental problems; *freedom* from a physical problem; *freedom* to be able to run like the wind with no restraint; *freedom* from the burden of debt; *freedom* from when your children grow up leaving you free to get on with another stage in your life; *freedom* for the right to chose; *freedom* from tyranny, and on and on and on...
Freedom can take many forms. But what Don Juan Matus was really talking about was freedom of the *soul*, freedom from the earth with all its desires.

Desires alone can be wonderful: love (not the unconditional kind), sex, food, drink, a little gambling (just for fun you understand), spirituality (yes, even that), religion. Given *balance* EVERYTHING is okay. But to attain balance is another thing.

Don Juan spent his whole life (lives?) attaining discipline and *balance*. In the end he was glad to leave. Not that he disliked Mother Earth, but it was too *restricting* for him. He had had enough of this 3-dimensional reality. Although, of course, unlike other men, he had access to a myriad of *other worlds* but he had had enough! It was *his time to go and NOT return!* He *chose* not to return.

Don Juan never pretended to be other than what he was. He never competed against another man, he didn't have to, besides that was not his way.

He had a way of teaching that scared the hell

out of his apprentice, Carlos Castaneda. Yet he chose Carlos as his successor. Why? Because he *knew* Carlos had the makings of a fine sorcerer or spiritual master, even though Carlos hadn't the foggiest idea of what he was letting himself in for.

Carlos used to write notes incessantly. This annoyed and amused Don Juan. Carlos carried his note-pad everywhere. It was an amusing bone of contention. Until Carlos was enough of a *Spiritual Warrior*, or *Man of Knowledge*, to dispense with it, then he learned to retain his memory in minute detail.

Don Juan had a further reason for choosing Carlos Castaneda: he could *write*. Boy, could he write.

Me? I'm still working on my own personal *freedom*. But I'm getting there, I'm getting there!

FORGIVENESS.

The word 'forgiveness' is used on many levels: spiritual, psychoanalytically and social, as a sort of 'give away' word like: "I'll never forgive you for that!" or "I can forgive you quite easily". Neither of these examples of 'forgiving' is quite up to scratch. Try the psychoanalyst's approach: "You have to forgive yourself first or nothing works!" Well, that's nearer the mark.

Forgiveness is *very* hard to actually carry out. I mean you can say: "I forgive you," but if you don't *mean* it then it will re-appear, raise its ugly head in that *very* same attitude. That person can then 'pick up' whether you have forgiven them or not. I'm not saying that it's *easy*, oh no. But you have to work at it.

The *Shrink's* approach of "You have to forgive yourSELF first" is in fact quite true. Forgiveness of the Self is like *loving* ones self: if you can't love yourself than you can't possibly love someone else. By 'love' I mean the uncompromising kind, without conditions attached to it. *Unconditional.*

Forgiveness starts from the heart, not from the head. It CAN start from the head, however, but *has* to work itself down to the heart and *out* from the heart.

Mahatma Ghandi *forgave* his assassin *immediately* after he felt the bullet! The Mahatma, you may say, was an extraordinary man. Another *extraordinary man* was Jesus: "Forgive them Father for they know not what they do." They were *crucifying* him!

The *Watcher* plays a part in all of this. What, or who, is the *Watcher?* The *Watcher* is that part of the Self that observes all that is going on. The *Watcher* is the 'built in' analyst. How can you get in touch with the *Watcher?* You can do it right away, if you like.

As you read this piece, unless you are totally absorbed and *living in the moment* (and I hope that many of you are), your thoughts are probably elsewhere, only 70% reading and understanding this piece, 30% is somewhere else thinking of what else you have to do, what else you have to acquire, where else you have to go (or be), who else you have to see, etc. But there is a part of you that is Watching and observing ALL that you do. It is *not* separate from you, but is the *real* you.

During the quiet of meditation, when the mind is still, there is a gentle part of you that *Watches*, it is always gentle, never angry, never agitated, never upset in any way, this then is the *Watcher.* As you concentrate your mind on the *Watcher* you BECOME the *Watcher*. For that is who you really are! You are not the ego, that chattering monkey always seeking, demanding attention, you are not jealousy, nor envy, nor possessiveness, nor anger. You think *that* is the real you but you are mistaken, the real you is that pinprick of consciousness that only on occasion bubbles to the surface. The more you concentrate on the *Watcher* the more REAL it becomes because it IS reality, true reality, not the "why did I do that?" or "why did I say that, I didn't mean it?" or further, "why am I *thinking* that?" Well, don't go beating yourself up about it. It's just a thought. "But then," you might reply to yourself, "then why did I think it in the first place?" Let it go! Let it run its course and LET IT GO! Just notice it, BUT DON'T SHRINK FROM IT, don't hide from it. Let it come, be the *Watcher* of it, the observer. But do not under any circumstance be drawn into it. That's the secret.

Acceptance can be very valuable too. Accept what you see and feel. You may have feelings of guilt but it is only a *thought form* come to tempt you. Once you have gone past this period (and we ALL have them) you will feel the serenity of the *Watcher*. It's a weird thing but *you* tempt YOURSELF with all this stuff!

Some things, seemingly, are unforgivable: the senseless slaughter of a child, the murder of a helpless, defenceless, elderly person. That's when the sense of the *Eternal* and eternity come into play. You have to believe that life is a continuation of consciousness, that life *is* eternal, because it *is*. It takes a person like the Mahatma to *truly* forgive his murderer AND MEAN IT, as I've already said: don't beat your self up about it, just be aware of the *Watcher* and then you will not *need* to be *in* the position of being forgiven and having to forgive. The more you get in touch with the *Watcher* (the Witness) the more you *become* the *Watcher*, or the Higher Self.

If every person on this planet were to forgive everybody else there would be no wars, no famine, no disease, no crime. Everybody would share their knowledge, not covert it, there would be laughter echoing throughout the cosmos and that laughter would come from a little planet called Earth where the word *forgiveness* doesn't even exist, where it has no meaning because *everybody* would be in touch with their Higher Selves, their God Selves. And the adventure called *life* will not end there, for the end is endless, the adventure will start from *that* moment, that timeless moment when *love* truly enters the heart.

EPILEPSY

I joined *The Samaritans*. I reasoned that if I couldn't walk too well at least I could pick up a phone and *listen*. I did the training to see if I was the right temperament for the job, and the right *person* for the job. You see, *I* didn't think I could do it. Oh yes, I could speak to people and I could do my share of *listening*, which was half the job. But what about my EGO, was my ego telling me that: *"let everybody know that you are a Samaritan, that you HELP people?"* And *"what a good person I was?"* This troubled me. Was I doing it for the right reasons? Was I doing it for the right *moral* reasons?

Then the phone in the Samaritan office rang. It was my first call and I was urged to answer it by my fellow, more experienced, colleagues. I picked up the phone: "Hello, the Samaritans. Can I help you?" There was silence, then a huge sob that nearly broke my heart in two. She had family problems, HUGE family problems and needed someone to offload on. I listened and I listened, putting in a sympathetic 'yes' and 'no' here and there, and the occasional 'aha'. Then she brightened up. Made a decision as to what she was going to do, thanked me for *"listening and all that I had done"* and hung up.

Never once during that call did I think that I was doing her a huge favour. Never once during that call did I think *anything* only my concern for the client. I had passed my own personal test!

During my nine years with the *Samaritans* I became what is known in the Samaritan trade as a *day leader*. In other words I had to stay within reach of my telephone in case certain decisions had to be made, and then it's down to me to take responsibility for that decision, usually concerning a client. Like, do we drive out (flying squad) to see a client if they need a home visit? Maybe that client had a history of violence when they had had a drink. Or maybe they were just wasting our time. Nine times out of ten I would say "yes, call the flying squad" (those Samaritans who are nearest the client who will get called out whether they like it or not). Of course they are not *pressed* into going, and maybe they're just *not in*, or are just about to pick up the kids from school, and like that. But usually someone (an old, reliable trooper) would be found.

But I held firm on not becoming a *group leader*. That area involved the *politics* of the Samaritans. That wasn't for me. But I WAS interested in training new recruits. Part of this training concerned acting out the part of *Samaritan and client*. As a radio actor this was right up my alley. But before we tried it out on the prospective *new* recruits we tried acting it out with just the director of the local branch of the Sams and a Group Leader. The Group Leader took the part of the Samaritan and I took the part of the client: with me crying, snot running down my face as well as tears, angry one minute and in denial the next, swearing like a trooper and then apologising profusely. Me taking the part of an epileptic with no job "I might just as well hang a *!"*^"!! sign round my bloody neck saying *epileptic*," I wailed.

I finished my performance by quietening down and accepting the offer of the cup of coffee that she had offered me at the beginning of the interview. The GL was open-mouthed. The director had thought that we had tapped something deep within me that I just *had* to let out. I looked at them and burst out laughing. "I'm an actor," I said, "that is what I *do*!"

Then we had to do it in front of the raw recruits. The director couldn't watch. Instead he sat on the stairs OUTSIDE of the room, his back to the door. Or maybe he was just too embarrassed?

During my 9-year stay with the Sams I met some people who in my eyes are HEROES, people who you could call on, day or night, to come out and deal with some poor soul. Or just *listen*. People you could *rely* on in a crisis. People who were full of compassion and love, yet knew when to be tough, when it was appropriate to be firm. Yet in their firmness and toughness there was LOVE working. Always working.

I met Paul Booth there. He was a fellow polio person. But he was in a wheelchair where I could walk. He was of the Baha'i faith. In between calls we would talk. He on what motivated him and I on what motivated me. We *always* spoke of the Power of Love. We sometimes spoke of psychic matters.

Many years later we met up again. We had both moved to Sussex, he to Uckfield and I to Lancing. We had a standing joke that he (I being a veggie) would always have a cauliflower cheese in the oven, no matter what. And guess what? When I visited him in Uckfield we had cauliflower cheese! It must have been in his oven for *years*!

He was a good worker for his faith, and dedicated his life to the Baha'is. After I had finished the cauliflower cheese it took me ten minutes to figure out how to stand up! Not because of the vast meal but he only had one chair that I could sit on...and it was a *low* chair. Through the years I, like him, had deteriorated, the curse of *Post Polio Syndrome*. I eventually managed to haul myself up, said my goodbyes, and was off.

The last phone call I had from him was in Wales. He had cancer of the liver. There was nothing anyone could do. But the nurses were absolutely amazed. They expected him to be the colour of a banana and in considerable pain. But the weight of healing prayer sent out to him, that and his 'Chinese Herbs' kept it at bay. He lost the fight, however. He was becoming weaker and had to be hospitalised, but still no pain. He died peacefully in his sleep.

I got a call from his sister Wendy. I *knew* that he had gone. After the call I went to bed and turned the light off.

I just KNEW that he was there! I tuned in. And there he was, standing up now for the first time in his polio ridden life. He stood about 5' 10", though I couldn't see his legs. "Tell Wendy that I'm *so* happy. Will you do that for me, Paul? I'm SO happy. I knew that you were the person for the job." He took my hand (I felt nothing physically but I *know* when someone takes my hand) and I instigated a hug. He responded. The tears came then. He left me. But there was, so very far away, if you can measure distance in a situation like that, a heavily bearded man wearing a turban and robe. I got the impression that he had brought Paul to see me.

I wrote to Paul's sister and told her what had happened. I sent the letter to Paul's address, as I had no other. Wendy rang me. She had been at Paul's place to clear up and had opened my letter beneath the picture of the now leader of the Baha'i faith. This leader wore a turban and a robe and was heavily bearded. Wendy was also of the Ba'hi faith.

These years later, after the brain tumour was removed, I became a *real* epileptic. The tumour was the size of an orange. Benign, thank god, a meningioma type. The epilepsy was treated with drugs, sort of 'chemical insulation tape' to prevent the electricity in my brain from 'sparking over'. When I do have a 'fit' it's like being plugged into the mains. I have a 30 to 40 second warning. If deep breathing doesn't ward it off (which is rare) then I lie on my right side and let it happen. THERE IS ABSOLUTELY NOTHING I CAN DO ABOUT IT. I go into spasm: my head jerking uncontrollably, pulled round to the right. My eyes roll and my right arm goes walkabout. It lasts for between five and six minutes. I'm conscious all the time but cannot speak, my breathing making a strange, slobbering sound. Crazy as it sounds but my mind, or consciousness, remains calm and reassuring, like the eye of a storm, repeating over and over: "*It'll soon be over. You just have to ride it out*! Yet it's horrible. And that's an understatement. There is no control what so ever. And when it's over I cannot speak and my arm is paralysed. Gradually, over half an hour to an hour I regain normal speech and the arm gathers strength. It's rather like a spark plug that is arcing over, the wire having worn thin, the outer insulation temporally gone. The engine will not function properly unless something is done about the *insulation*, in my case *chemical insulation*. More drugs? Well not always. It's taken nearly three and a half years to get the balance right. I changed from the drug phenytoin to tegretol. But that's another story.

I've often thought of my father when an operation for a duodenal ulcer went wrong and a clot of blood went to his brain causing a paralysis of his left arm and the side of his face, the strength in his arm was there, only he just couldn't *feel* to touch. He too became epileptic. I vividly remember him being stretchered out by two ambulance men through our little seaside fish restaurant in Herne Bay. He was screaming wildly and grabbing on to anything that came to hand. So they had to strap him down. Again they controlled his fits with drugs.

My father took to drink to drown out the fact that he was once a very athletic man, an ex-professional wrestler. When he drank he was no longer the father I once knew and respected. I knew that he was suffering. But I also knew that he could and *did* throw *fake* fits. He was an expert at '*Pratt falls*' and could throw himself on the floor and fake a fit just to get attention. I remember saying at just 14 years old that he'd "lost his self respect". He'd steal money from the restaurant till just so that he could get smashed down the pub. Again and again he'd promise that he'd give it up. But never did. Then we had an argument, he and I. Over what, I don't remember. He threw one of his fake fits. I just stepped over him and went out the room. But WAS it a fake fit? I shall never know for sure. Perhaps *that's* why I chose epilepsy as my subject for the "client" acting as an epileptic? Maybe I felt such guilt at stepping over my father and leaving the room that it all came back in my acting scenario! I don't know and never WILL know, at least not in *this* life.

My mother and father divorced after he had an affair with my mother's best friend. He got her pregnant. My mother also found out that he had cheated at cards: marking the cards (Grandfather Bura was a professional gambler and taught his sons all the tricks of the trade). She had thought it odd that his close friends and business associates didn't call anymore and socialise. This incident was BEFORE his operation.

When my father died he came to me during a musical meditation and asked for my forgiveness. He was kneeling down on his haunches (an idiosyncratic habit when he had something important to say). I answered him by saying: "I only wish I could have loved you more, dad, and there really is nothing to forgive on my part. Complete your journey and go with god." He smiled and was gone. Even that, on reflection later, was a bit pious. But I'm absolutely *sure* that he did. Sure that I made him just that little bit happier on his final journey!

THE BLUE POND

The being of pure light set it free, casting it out over the ethers like a line attached to a fishing rod, throwing it out and away into the round, Blue Pond, glistening and glowing in the light of the sun. As it plopped into the waters it rippled awhile; then out, thus causing the effect of freedom, for it *was* free! It swam ashore and so entered the thick, gluey substance that was to become its home once more.

He would have little memory of this, no template on which to build the experience. He would grow up in a family that was poor but happy, parents that had a basis, a foundation of *kindness* and *balance* but above all *love*: love for *all* creatures, all sentient beings.

He took to this life quite easily, took to this *way of life*, responded to it and grew up to be a Man of Compassion and Wisdom, a wisdom that grew in him without any effort on his part, seemingly, for that is what he *was*. But then he was not aware of what had gone before.

He did not know *when* he would meet the Madman but meet him he would: around any corner; in any town or village; any place. But when he did meet him he would *know*.

He met the Madman on a dusty road between nowhere and somewhere carrying an axe, the Madman actually tried to kill him! With a cry of pain this Madman, so full of hate, tried to axe the Man, the Man who knew only kindness and love, the Man who would rather sacrifice *himself* rather than cause another pain. The Man was puzzled and dodged the blow. Again this Madman aimed his axe at the Man's head but again he fended off the blow. The Madman grew even madder and aimed blow after blow at the Man. The Man again danced nimbly sideways. The Madman was now in a state of fatigue blowing hard as the axe became heavier. Every time he aimed the axe it fell short, and every time the axe would *grow* in weight. The Madman became exhausted but would not give up; the hate in him fuelled his strength.

At last he gave up the assault. Foaming at the mouth he heaped curse after curse upon the Man until even the cursing exhausted him. "Why do you do this?" asked the Man, softly. "Because your light hurts my eyes and offends me!" he rasped, completely breathless. "That is not logical," said the Man. "Must everything be logical to you? Do you not understand? Your light hurts my eyes your voice drives me to madness. I *must* destroy you!" said the Madman. "Who are you that you must do this thing?" asked the Man. "I have come to annihilate you, to kill you and all *like* you," the Madman replied. The Man walked forward to embrace the Madman. "Stay away from me, stay away!" He raised his axe once more. There was fear and terror in the Madman's eyes for the first time. "Why are you afraid of the light?" said the Man. "Why?" cried the Madman, " I don't *know* why. I think *you* know the answer to that better than I."

The Man touched the Madman. The Madman drew back as if scalded. Instantly a black shadow swarmed out of the Madman's mouth. It grew and grew until it filled the skies with darkness. Thunder stood about it and above it, lightning leapt from its black heart.

The Man stood and raised his arms to the heavens. "I welcome you, brother, as I welcome all creation. You are no more evil than the host that you inhabited. Where is the fear in you, where is the fear in *me*? Where is the soul that sent you? Is it not as pure as *my* soul? Is it not a spark of the Eternal One as my soul is? Is not the line that *your* soul, HIS soul –pointing at the madman- thrown into the Blue Pond as real as mine? And *still* it has a hold of you. Yet you refuse to be reeled in until you have caused as much havoc, had as much so-called fun as you can. Don't you understand? *You* will be reeled in eventually, even if it takes a billion years, you have nowhere to run to...except to the One who created you; for whether you like it or not, you ARE created just as I am, but *not* by the Infinite. You cannot destroy me anymore than I can destroy you! You, my friend, have chosen IMBALANCE and hate, that is HE has chosen (indicating the Madman), I have chosen BALANCE and love, for that is *our true nature*. In the end of things, and there IS no end, you have to choose, you will have to choose whether you wish to stay down here and DESTROY everything with hate until there is nothing left to destroy, or to EMBRACE everything with love, compassion and learning. In the end, my friend, love is all there is. All else is an illusion, a lesser reality." The Man was seen to be speaking to the madman AND the darkness that the Madman had created.

The Man waited for a response. Then with a terrible voice the darkness answered: "You think that you can trick *me* the master of darkness? Do you think that I am stupid? The shining one who sent me is a baby who knows NOTHING. I am as intelligent, beautiful, indestructible, clever and forthright as ever *you* are, or as ever the shining one who sent *us* is. There are millions of my kind ready and waiting to do my bidding. As you so rightly say: there IS no end, no end to what I can destroy, no end to what I can possess and own, no end to pain."

The Man waited for this tirade to end: "Then answer me this: *what are you afraid of?"* "Me? Afraid? What have I got to be afraid of?"

"**Me**."
"**You?**" the darkness replied, "**YOU?** Don't make me laugh!" The Man continued: "When you were inside the body of the Madman you were afraid to look at me, wouldn't even allow me to touch you."
"That wasn't *me* that was the Madman whom I inhabited," replied the darkness. "Then how is it that the so-called Madman is *no longer* afraid of me?"

The Madman now had cleared his senses; the darkness had receded and no longer invaded his body. This so-called Madman had been the servant of the darkness for many years and had killed in his name, raped in his name, tortured in his name. This same Madman had a soul too, a soul like any other: bright and shining, a droplet of the divine who had cast his rod and line, too, into the Blue Pond, but it had become caught up, tangled on the rocks of life over many aeons by the worship of the negative forces. Never had a shining one got anywhere *near* to him in so *many* lifetimes, not least *touched* him!

Now he was free: the weight that he carried, all the negativity simply fell away. The being that he had built up over many lifetimes had left him. It was the warm and compassionate touch of the Man, the touch that carried with it *no judgement* and no blame, only love.

Now the man focused his gaze on the ever-darkening cloud that fizzed and crackled and gave off a stench that was overpowering. This cloud had been IN the so-called Madman and now was an entity unto itself, a powerful *Thought Form* that was as real as you or I.

In its heart of hearts the darkness *knew* that it was no match against the light of the Man, yet it refused to let go. It tried to re-enter the so-called Madman but the arms of the Man were about him and regenerated the Madman's strength and sense of compassion, enough to fend off the attack for re-entry. The so-called Madman's strength was low but he had the *will*, he had felt *freedom* for the first time in all his lives, and he knew he was *loved, really* loved, and oh how that raised his spirit. But he had to fight *on his own* now, the Man's strength had filled him with an energy that he had never known and he was fighting *on his own* now!

He was being torn to shreds yet he knew that to resist was pointless, but this time he had *love* and *compassion* on his side, an awakening given to him by the Man.

"What is this?" the darkness thundered, "you cannot resist ME, I who *made* you, I who corrupted you so deliciously!" "You can no longer corrupt me because I AM INCORRUPTABLE," the Madman screamed, though the fear was still in him, "I *created* YOU, can't you understand that?" "If *you* created *me* then I am an *extension* of you and therefore I am your MASTER," the darkness replied, "and as your master I order you to LET ME IN!" "You are no longer my master, I created you and therefore I must..." the Madman hesitated, he wanted to say 'destroy you' but the words would not come out. "I must...must...LOVE YOU!"

The Madman had said the word, the word that he *never* thought he would say. "What? What did you say?!" The darkness began to shrink back into itself. The Madman had found new strength ON HIS OWN, the strength that was *his* from the beginning of the beginning, when he was first brought forth and cast into the Blue Pond as a fledgling extension of the one who sent him. The memory came back to him: oh, the Blue Pond had excited him, intoxicated him with its desires and he had eaten up those desires, quenched his thirst in them...but he had wanted MORE! His free will had allowed him *more*. But he had to hurt people to get *more* and the hurting of people became even more than his desire for *more;* his greed for more of everything. He *forgot* the gentle touch, he *forgot* about the balance of all things, *forgot* about the REAL meaning of love. Love to him was *taking* and not *giving*, he *forgot* about all of these things. How could he have been so stupid, so selfish?

All these things passed by him in a nanosecond, he HAD to do something about this monster that he had created and was responsible for. Then he said, when all was raging about him like some ghastly whirlpool of garbage, he said quite softly, almost inaudibly, but with the force of *all* his being, all his *intent*, the words: *I Love You*. Then again but with more force: *I LOVE YOU!*

He aimed these powerful words *at* the ugly vortex raging about him. A small part of him still wanted the power of this hurricane-like force but instantly he *knew* that to go back was the way to *true* insanity. The label 'Madman' that he had earned was only a small part of what he would become if he gave in to this hideousness that he had made. The truth was the Man *loved* him even as he *was*, THAT was the difference. The Man saw in him the bright, shining labyrinth of glory that was his *birthright*.

The Madman had come to his senses. He wasn't the 'Madman' anymore. Suddenly he was filled with ecstasy and a 'knowing'. The darkness shrank from him even more. The darkness 'knew' now what this Madman 'knew' and although fighting till the last, dropped down from the skies.

Instantly, there was a stillness, a silence so profound as to hear a single feather drop from a nest. Then an *incredible* thing occurred: the darkness became a blinding light, a sacred, blazing ladder, that reached high up into the heavens and from this fiery ladder a beautiful being, neither male nor female, descended, so graceful was it that it almost floated.

It was the madman's soul *manifesting*, the soul that had cast him into the Blue Pond time and time again, thousands of years before. This Higher Being spoke with a voice so beautiful that the Madman wept.

"It is finished, Yarni, for that is your *soul name*, you came here as an aspect of me, and the Goddess of the Blue Pond made you welcome, very welcome. She bestowed upon you all of the Blue Pond's gifts. But therein lay the danger: you wanted MORE, and, as the recipient of *free will*, you *got* more, and the more you had the more you wanted.

But you *know* all of that now. This is *not* the reason that I sent you. The real reason was to *set you free* to experience all there is to know in the Blue Pond. Once you had gathered it you forgot all about me, forgot to report back to the person who sent you, because you had forgotten how and the *purpose* of which you came. Of all the millions of souls YOU were chosen as a leader, to lead mankind into the light, instead you led them into darkness. But I have not revealed myself to judge you. There *is* no judgement, no hell, no anything...except LOVE and the *free will* to use it...or not. All else is an illusion. For in *love* there is EVERYTHING. Lovers fall *IN LOVE*, you too *FALL IN TO LOVE*. Lovers experience ecstasy, which soon fades. You will experience ecstasy and *completeness* that NEVER fades because you ARE ecstasy, you ARE completeness, you ARE love. ALL is One."

The Madman, from now on to be called *Yarni*, dried his tears. As he did so the Man vanished, never to be seen again. And to think that Yarni had tried to kill him with an axe; the Man, Yarnie now realised, was *sent* to him on a mission and now his mission was complete the Man stepped *out* of the Blue Pond. "Somehow," Yarni thought, "I will see him again for I owe him so much." "You owe me *nothing*," the voice seem to come out of the very air, the voice that the Man had used to such effect, "for now you are on your own."

Yarni stood silently waiting for the voice to say more, then he realised with complete amazement that the voice of the Man AND the Being of Light were the same. Such a puzzle. Then came the thought: *yet another aspect of the same being?* "Ah, yes," he said out loud, "ah, yes."

The clouds of unreason were beginning to disperse at last. NOW it would begin!

FINDING THE BALANCE

Dignity finds its own balance with the individual self. It is only an *expression* of self. We all need a piece of dignity to function in this world, just as we also need a piece of ego. They all find their own level of function, their own *balance*.

When I was 7-years-old and caught polio this left me with withered legs (my left leg more than my right), a beer belly because I had lost my tummy muscles, my right arm was thin but my left arm normal. I had a double curvature of the spine resulting in my having to wear a spinal brace.

When I reached 13 I started taking notice of girls. I was asked to strip off in front of the doctors and nurses. I didn't mind that. They were all *old* and getting on a bit. But I *did* mind stripping off in front of a 17-year-old student nurse who was rather attractive! I was too young to know anything about *dignity* and how it functioned. I wanted to look, well, *normal*, in front of this pretty nurse. And there was I, almost in the buff, looking like a young (good looking?) Quasimodo, and there was she looking like a beautiful Esmerelda. I didn't know where to hide!

Later on, I learned that you don't have to walk straight, don't have to have a fabulous body, in order to 'turn heads'. What you *do* need is a sense of humour and character that causes you to laugh at what the *eternal* has dished out to you. A *don't care* attitude. You have no choice but to develop this.

Dignity works on ALL levels. "Walk tall and with *dignity*," I hear the writers say. I need *dignity* to walk at all! Well, not *that* much.

Bring out *dignity* and brush it off for special occasions. But don't let it chain you, nor enslave you. Remember *balance* in *all* things. Otherwise you fall over!

DO NOT FOLLOW WHERE THE PATH MAY LEAD

"Do not follow where the path may lead, go instead where there is no path and leave a trail."

We have been trying to do that all our lives, haven't we? Yet I cannot find a *new* philosophy, a *new* trail.

Perhaps we're being too hard on ourselves. Our life *is* our trail. And if we can leave some markers along the way, some scrapings of love through this tangle, this jungle of a life, then we have succeeded.

But how do we begin? By doing the best job that we can, no matter how long it takes. I have been a writer of poetry and prose all my adult life and I like to think that I've improved. Some say that they think my old stuff is the *real* me, that I haven't really improved at all. Others say that I'm now in my stride. But no matter what people may think I'm continuing to leave poems along the trail of my life *like so many leaves*, some good, some rotten.

No matter what path we may choose, whether it be an actor, painter, a brickie, a carver in wood, a dustman (they leave their own trails along *our* paths. Only kidding, fellers), a clerk, a computer expert, a sewer man, or in the Services, *all*, all of you have to just apply a little thought, a little reason, and a little *love.*

And if you are unhappy in your chosen profession, look to another. You *can* do it. But you need a little love to grease the wheels of your life. If you have been applying love in your life, then what goes around comes around. Sometimes it's instant karma; sometimes it's not. I've said it before that *Time* equates as *change*. *Time* is a substance that is as slippery as an eel and slips through ones fingers again and again. But time is what we measure things and events by; time is of the *earth*. It doesn't exist in other dimensions. At least not as *we* know it. (Earthbound entities can sleep for what they term as a few hours, and WEEKS have flown by. They move so fast in their frequency and *we* move so slowly). As long as you do the best job that you know how and that applies to your social life too: how you treat people, especially your family and friends.

You don't have to be a genius and get bound up with 'being the best'. Sometimes second best is good too, even third best, or fourth best, as long as you *do your best*, the best you know how.

And you don't have to be a 'goody two-shoes' either. Let your hair down occasionally and hang loose (they can't touch you for it!). As long as you are *there* for folk, as long as you have time to *listen.*

Even if you don't know what their talking about. Just **be** there. A hug can go a long way to procuring a cure.

In the end love is all there is. We are all *different human beings* so therefore we all leave a different trail, no matter what.

It's taken me two and a bit pages to come to that conclusion, but I got there in the end.

DON'T TRUST ME, I'M A PSYCHIC

Just because I get things *right*, just because I can read the future sometimes, does not mean that I get it right *all of the time!* Sure, I can do a reading and I can score pretty heavily, but *not all of the time!* I can go into *Light Trance* and my voice and face can *and do* change, and sometimes the entity can come on really strong and I don't really know what I'm saying and I come out of the *trance state* and be presented with a client who is either weeping with emotion or wide-eyed with amazement, but *not all of the time!!*

I admire psychics who can get it right *all of the time!* But psychics like that are few and far between. I admire *dowsers* who appear to *get it right,* but name me one dowser who gets it right *all of the time.*

I have a small gift as a dowser (Read *QUEST FOR CONTACT* and *STEPPING TO THE DRUMMER*) but I don't pretend that I can get it right *all of the time;* It takes a will-of-iron and total separation from all thought to be a good dowser.

Psychics and dowsers have much in common. We work much better when we work *BLIND,* that is, we don't know beforehand anything about the subject we're *looking* at or *dowsing* for. Apart from a few preliminary pointers, our *psychic screens are clear.*

A case in point. I went to a house in a village in East Sussex that had been experiencing strange happenings: when they went out for the evening the house lights were, naturally enough, switched off. When they returned *all* the lights were blazing, the TV switched itself on and off. Then a footprint of a small person, probably a child, could be seen etched into the kitchen carpet, which no amount of bleach would remove and they felt as though they were *being watched!* At no time did they think it was evil in any way...just uncomfortable.

I, and a couple of friends, decided to visit the house and meet the family. They showed us the *footprint* and spoke in general about the phenomena. I then 'tuned in' and channelled an entity that spoke of having died in a fire with his small son. I explained to this *man* (mentally) what he would have to do: *to look for a point of light or lighted door* and *enter it with his son,* assuring him that all would be well. The *man* was SO distressed and had been trying to attract the family's attention to their dilemma. He thanked me and left.

The footprint? The footprint disappeared as suddenly as it had made itself known.

I should point out that the *in-between world*, which this man and his son had occupied, was a kind of 'timeless zone'. As far as this man was concerned only a couple of months had gone by! In reality, three-dimensional reality, *they*, the man and his son, were occupying FOURTH dimensional reality and

ONE HUNDRED YEARS HAD PASSED!

On checking the village church records, they found that a man and his small son had perished in a fire *on that very site* where the house was built.

But I don't get it right 'all of the time'. I remember when *The Seventh Sword* by Andrew Collins was published. Six of the swords had been found, but during the time period of *The Seventh Sword* going to print the Seventh Sword was found! Now I wasn't to know that. We were sitting, my friends and I, in meditation when I suddenly had a picture of where the Seventh Sword might be. I was seeing a wooded area by the side of which ran a river that curved round to the left, and then off to the right. Over the river was a railway, so it had to be a bridge of some kind. Suddenly one of my colleagues said *EPSOM*, what I had described was in Epsom in Surry. We pulled out an Ordnance Survey map of Surry and found Epsom. There was indeed a wooded area and a railway bridge, but no river. But the *old Well* at Epsom was still there, and curiously enough it had the number '7' on it.

My nephew Quenton and the Porthouse brothers, Mark and Jason, decided to pay Epson a visit. So loading up the metal detector and a flask of soup we headed toward Epson from Lancing in Sussex.

We found the *Old Well* with the number '7' atop it (the Epson Well from where the famous Epson salts originated) right in the middle of a brand new housing estate. We enquired at various house as to why the number 7 was put on the top of the well. Nobody knew (Of course there *had* to be an explanation!). We spread the map out on the bonnet of my car and map-doused for the sword, we picked up a *Courier Line* around the Well (an energy line that carries information *to* and *fro*) and found on the map that it ran straight through the wooded area with the railway that I had *seen* in my original vision.

We arrived at the railway bridge that had a wooded area running to the side of it. We drove down a small road and there in front of us was a small stream, which curved to the left, and then to the right, *it went directly UNDER the railway bridge!* We spoke to an old gentleman cutting his hedge. "Do you know anything about this stream?" "Indeed I do," he said, " it was once a small river until the Water Board got its hands on it. Now it's a mere stream," he said with disgust.

We drove over a small bridge that straddled the stream, and stopped just short of the wooded area. The boys got out, and having got me into my wheeled steed, clutching the flask of soup, and, carrying the metal detector, we set off.

In my original vision I saw a felled tree. We too saw a felled tree, old and rotten now. The lads set to work with the metal detector whilst I looked on. Every now and then they stopped for a 'soup break' (I had made the soup out of onions thickened with chickpea flour with a teaspoon of Patax Chilli Pickle. It was delicious and I have made it many times since. I've named it *Seventh Sword Soup* out of respect for the quest). The lads worked hard. But we found NOTHING!

All the pieces had fitted together: the railway bridge; the stream (once a river) that curved *exactly* the way I saw it in my vision; the little wooded area; the fallen tree; even the number 7 atop the Epsom Well, from where we had doused a line that lead us to the wooded area, YET THE SWORD HAD ALREADY BEEN FOUND! *Now, what was THAT all about?* Your guess is as good as mine.

Being a psychic is a serious business. But one shouldn't take your self too seriously, though. It's not an exact science. But the time will come when *everybody* will be their OWN psychic, when the past present and the future will all blend into a glorious whole. For you will *know* where you are going: neither commerce or remembering to put the cat out will matter, worrying about paying the mortgage on time will not matter, fear of dying will not matter for you *cannot* die!

I can predict with surety that we're heading for a *CHANGE* that will blow your socks off, a change so dramatic yet so profound as to shake the very fabric of your being AND the Being of this planet! Yet all of this is happening INSIDE of you, INSIDE this planet, NOW!

The planet Earth has already started *Her* change, clawing her way up the frequencies. Time, as you have already noticed, is speeding up; the weather is changing; nature is beginning to change; the ice caps are beginning to melt far more quickly than science could predict; animal species are dying out at in incredible rate. It's a roller coaster of a ride in terms of the Earths history!

All the guilt, all the fear, will evaporate. I'm not talking about a new religion here, religion will go the way of most things, most organisations: crumbling into dust leaving only the spirit of the inner light to guide the way.

The great religions *almost* got it right. But then they added *fear* into the equation, fear and *power* and the need to *hold on to everything.* Man started tampering with the scriptures: a little edit here and a little edit there. They even started to ADD their *own* material so the church could have more power over man/womankind. Even in India where Holy Men can be found by the thousand on every street corner. A certain Guru stated that he *was* a God. His teachings appeared sound and inviting and he *appeared* to do miracles. Millions followed him and he conned them all by telling them what they all wanted to hear, his *spiritual flattery* was legendary; until he was found out and charged with obscenity and sexual deviation to gratify none but himself. But even one such as this should not be judged: the natural law of *cause and effect* will swing into play and come the day this Guru will put things right. All come from God and *all* will return, that's a promise with a rainbow wrapped around it. After all, we are *all* Gods in the making.

The law of LOVE is perfect but it takes no prisoners. FREEDOM is another word that roughly means the *same thing*. The law of Love/Freedom doesn't allow you to take any baggage with you on your journey to the Light, to the Source, to your own *Self*. Freedom means just that: FREEDOM. *He aint heavy, he's my brother/sister.* God carries you? Naw, you carry yourself into that Light that YOU created in the first place. Remember, *there aint no Time or Space that has a place,* because there *is* no place...ANYWHERE. You *are* the Light, you *are* Freedom, and you *are* Love right now! Nuff said?

NOTE: *First published by The Quarterly.*

CIRCLES OF CHANGE
(For all the 'croppies' out there)
In the cocoon of Infinity
A sun was born out of
The dust and swirl of Space,
A young sun full of the energy
And vitality of youth.

But soon it swelled with pride
For it too was to create a family,
A new family: a family of planets.

The young sun spat out its young:
 Cooling droplets in a sea of brilliance,
Surrounding itself with a new family
Of its own, a family to lavish and cherish,
But above all: to FEED.

It showered the young planets
With food, with prana,
Life giving droplets of pure energy,
And like the human beings that were to follow
Each planet had its own character, its own identity.
And through the vastness of time
The planets too spawned LIFE,
And each planet had to find its own BALANCE.

*In the beginning of things
Were circles of pure energy,
Etched in the corn and herbs
Of that far off time.*

*That energy belonged to the earth.
We humans shared this energy
In wonderment and awe
Wondering, in our innocence,
What this strange power,
This energy that could 'change'
A man forever, could be?*

*So we built Stone Complexes
Upon this divine energy
In celebration, celebration
That the earth should give to us a gift,
Not yet realising that it was our divine right
As human beings, and prospective gods.*

*We were told
By the Wise Ones amongst us
That this energy was so precious
And so beautiful that in those days
We worshiped this energy.*

*This energy could foretell
Whether we would have a good harvest,*

Whether we would have storms
Whether those storms would tear down the crops
Which in turn taught us to store the surplus grain.

Through the advent of time
Those that were sensitive to the Earth mother
Learned to build with more sophistication
That would allow us to control even the weather.

There were those amongst us
Who tapped this energy
For the purpose of healing;
Plus the pursuit of a higher, more gentle knowledge.
The circles became
More sophisticated:
A henge within a henge
With a central spiral
Which became the Seat of Power
Which connected with lines
Of energy that also connected
With places that became holy,

And the Priests among them
Would sit in these Seats of Power
And the people would dance
Hand in hand amongst the stones,
Hand in hand they would dance in circles
This way and that in the places of power,

Thus increasing the energy.
The faster they danced and sang
The stronger the energy.
So strong was its power that they
Became intoxicated with it.
The priests, in their wisdom, limited their dancing
To once a month: and the full moon.

And the priests would sit in the Seat of Power
And when the energy was at its height
Would disappear, vanish, and when they reappeared
They told tales of peoples in other lands
And other similar Place's of Power
And of the way these other people lived.

This energy made the people more fertile
And they made love among the stones,
Building fires to keep them warm,
And the fire was a symbol
Of the fire in their loins.

And the wise amongst them learned how
To read the stars and how the stars
Seem to move and they set more stones
To signify these movements
And their effects on the minds of men.

*And it came to them by realisation and
experimentation
That each circle or pattern is of itself USELESS
Unless the elements of water are present
And earth energy to power it.
But above all there had to be SOUND.
And the sound through singing and chanting and
movement
Came to them easily.*

*The Wise ones noticed also
That this whirling around, this spinning
Was also reflected in nature:
Certain Devas whirl;
Elementals whirl;
Through special insight they came to realise
That even galaxies whirl and spin
Through the vastness of space;
Hurricanes whirl;
Sorcerers, just before disappearing,
Roar, whirl, and spin.*

*Each of us has within us
A pattern 'unique' to us,
When we fulfil that pattern
It changes into something else.
That 'something else' is our Evolving, Revolving Self,
That Evolving, Revolving Self is our destiny.*

Our Evolving, Revolving Self,
No matter what form it takes,
Affects other beings that come in contact with it.
Just as these patterns in the corn change YOU!

They change the surrounding countryside
In their very SHAPE, they change towns
And villages and make them WHAT THEY ARE.
YOU make them what they are.
YOU make a difference.

The constant chatter along
The lines that connect
EVERYTHING and EVERYONE
By our whirling chakras
Makes us WHO WE ARE..

And others who have
These lines and patterns
Change the patterns of others,
They cannot help themselves.
Resistance is pain, no matter
What that resistance may be.

But the circles have come again,
This time even more beautiful,
And even more complex in an age of complexity.

And in this age of complexity
We still want to know WHY?
Is it that we now have to look within?
Fed up with all the material things?

Are they saying to us:
LOOK AT THE CIRCLES
OF YOUR MIND, THEREIN
LAY THE ANSWERS?
YOU HAVE NOTHING TO LOSE
BUT A LITTLE FACE!

The Earth Goddess is writing
To us letters in the corn, messages.
And we cannot understand her!
But we do not HAVE to understand.
The Shapes themselves ARE the power,
The Shapes themselves ARE the reality.
Long ago, the people got intoxicated
With this energy, which in turn CHANGED
Their reality; opened them up to who they really
were!

That time is come again.
The circles not only affect us

But affect the whole of the countryside;
The whole of the earth.

And your mind screams back...
(Ah, your mind is forever screaming)
Well let it scream at the stars and moon
And will they shout back:
ARE YOU ARE A LOONEY-TUNE?

I think not.
You are the sum-total
Of all that's gone before,
And when you have settled the score
Will you STILL want more?

You will already own the earth
And all that's in it,
You will have it all, and more.
But above all you will be
At peace with your Self,
Now THAT'S wealth.

Peace, freedom and Love
They are all the same.

And when you are privileged
To wrap yourself in this sacred geometry,
Whether it be in an 'out-door temple'

Or the' in-door church',
Say to your Self:
I AM it, I AM the I AM
Without OWNING anything of it!

When finally you grow
Into a universe
Your humility will be complete
And you will have at last 'come home'.
Union with God will be yours.

But If the questions still persist:
Who am I?
What am I?
Where am I going?

Then maybe God will remain for you
Always the Great Mystery,
Still an enigma
And you will be as far
From the Truth as a million 'light years'
And yet be as near to it
As a single breath!

ABOUT THE AUTHOR

Paul Bura is a poet, writer and broadcaster. He produced many of the voices behind Thames Television's *Larry The Lamb* where he got his first break and subsequently embarked on a career as a Voice-Over artist. He went on to co-present BBC Radio.4's *SOUNDS WORDS AND MOVEMENT*. Then he moved to Channel 4's *SAME DIFFERENCE* as an on-screen reporter. He is the author of eight books of verse but not only writes poetry but is a regular contributor to magazines like *The Science of Thought Review (now 'New Vision'), The Quarterly, One Vision and SC Magazine (now* **swirlednews.com***)*. He also wrote with **Andy Thomas** the book *Quest for Contact* where his abilities as a psychic really came to the fore. His autobiographical book *STEPPING TO THE DRUMMER* 'The Extraordinary Tales of a Psychic Man', with a foreword by Uri Geller, brings it all together. He is a performing poet *"with a voice that would make Dylan Thomas growl in his grave with envy,"* thus said the writer and poet Christy Brown author of *Down All The Days* and *MY LEFT FOOT, subsequently made into a film starring* Daniel Day-Lewis. His latest book: **THE STRANGER ON THE THRESHOLD** is a collection of stories and essays on the subject of Love and Compassion. He is currently scripting the Letters of Christy Brown for BBC Radio.4. titled: **DEAR CHRISTY, DEAR PAUL** and has written, also for Radio.4. his childhood in the 50's: **THE LITTLE CAFÉ ON THE PROM,** an endearing, funny, and sometimes moving document of a lad that one day was running on two legs and the next screeching around corners in a wheelchair.

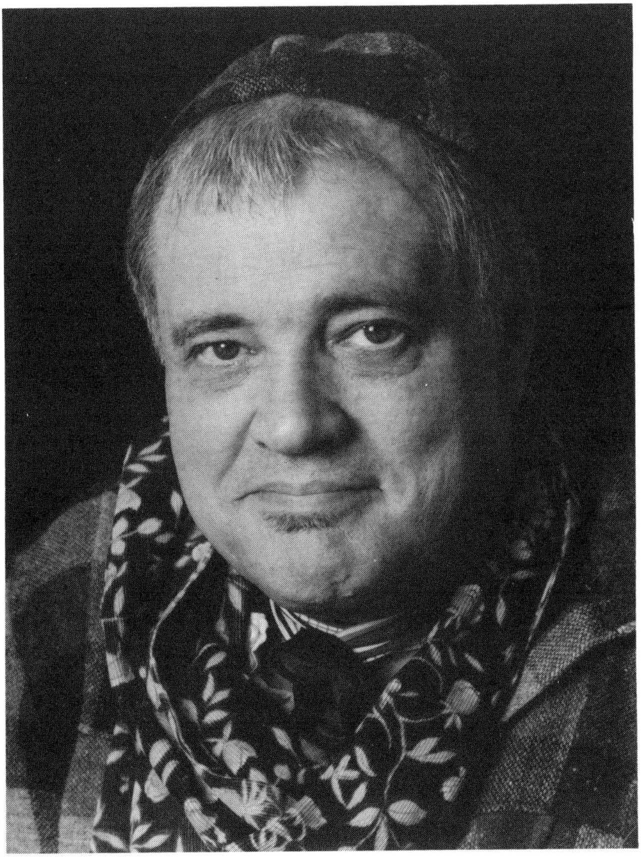